The Measure of a Christian

STUDIES IN JAMES 1

Gene A. Getz

Regal Books
A Division of GL Publications
Ventura, CA U.S.A.

Other Regal reading by Gene A. Getz:
  Abraham: Trials and Triumphs
  David: God's Man in Faith and Failure
  Joshua: Defeat to Victory
  Moses: Moments of Glory . . . Feet of Clay
  Nehemiah: A Man of Prayer and Persistence
  Joseph: From Prison to Palace

The foreign language publishing of all Regal books is under the direction of GLINT. GLINT provides financial and technical help for the adaptation, translation and publishing of books for millions of people worldwide. For information regarding translation contact: GLINT, P.O. Box 6688, Ventura, California 93006.

Scripture quotations in the publication are from the *New International Version*, Holy Bible. Copyright © 1973 and 1978 by New York International Bible Society. Used by permission.
Also quoted is the *NASB, New American Standard Bible*. © The Lockman Foundation 1960, 1962, 1963, 1968, 1971, 1972, 1973, 1975. Used by permission.

Published by Regal Books
A Division of GL Publications
Ventura, California 93006
Printed in U.S.A.

Library of Congress Cataloging in Publication Data
Getz, Gene A.
   The measure of a Christian.

   (The Measure of— series)
   Includes bibliographical references.
   1. Bible. N.T. James I—Criticism, interpretation, etc.
I. Bible. N.T. James. English. 1983.   II. Title.
III. Series.
BS2785.2.G47   1983   227'.9107   83-4440
ISBN 0-8307-0881-2

CONTENTS

WHY THIS STUDY?

Of all New Testament books, the epistle of James focuses on "developing the mind of Christ." Furthermore, it is intensely personal. Though much of what is written is directed to "believers in relationship," great portions of the letter are directed to individual Christians and what should characterize their personal life style.

If you'll let Him, the Holy Spirit will use this study to "renew your mind," enabling you to "test and prove what God's will is." And as you do, you'll be able to contribute significantly to helping your fellow Christians—*as a body* of believers—also develop the mind of Christ. In that sense, Paul's prayer for the Romans will be answered in your own church—"that with *one heart* and *mind* you may glorify the God and Father of our Lord Jesus Christ" (Rom. 15:5).

RENEWAL—A BIBLICAL PERSPECTIVE

Renewal is the essence of dynamic Christianity and the basis on which Christians, both in a corporate or "body" sense and as individual believers, can determine the will of God. Paul made this clear when he wrote to the Roman Christians—"be transformed by the *renewing of your mind*. Then" he continued "you will be able to test and prove what God's will is" (Rom. 12:2). Here Paul is talking about renewal in a corporate sense. In other words, Paul is asking these Christians as a *body* of believers, to develop the mind of Christ through corporate renewal.

Personal renewal will not happen as God intended it unless it happens in the context of corporate renewal. On the other hand, corporate renewal will not happen as God intended without personal renewal. Both are necessary.

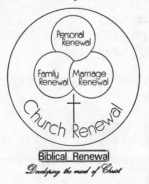

Biblical Renewal
Developing the mind of Christ

The larger circle represents "church renewal." This is the most comprehensive concept in the New Testament. However, every local church is made up of smaller self-contained, but interrelated units. The *family* in Scripture emerges as the "church in miniature." In turn, the family is made up of an even smaller social unit—*marriage*. The third inner circle represents *personal* renewal, which is inseparably linked to all of the other basic units. Marriage is made up of two separate individuals who become one. The family is made up of parents and children who are also to reflect the mind of Christ. And the church is made up of not only individual Christians, but couples and families.

Though all of these social units are interrelated, biblical renewal can begin within any specific social unit. But wherever it begins—in the church, families, marriages or individuals—the process immediately touches all the other social units. And one thing is certain! All that God says is consistent and harmonious. He does not have one set of principles for the church and another set for the family, another for husbands and wives and another for individual Christians. For example, the principles God outlines for local church elders, fathers and husbands regarding their role as leaders are interrelated and consistent. If they are not, we can be sure that we have not interpreted God's plan accurately.

The books listed below are part of the Biblical Renewal Series by Gene Getz designed to provide supportive help in moving toward renewal. They all fit into one of the circles described above and will provoke thought, provide interaction and tangible steps toward growth.

ONE ANOTHER SERIES	PERSONALITY SERIES	THE MEASURE OF SERIES
Building Up One Another	Abraham	Measure of a . . .
	David	Church
Encouraging One Another	Joseph	Family
	Joshua	Man
	Moses	Marriage
Loving One Another	Nehemiah	Woman
		Christian—Philippians
		Christian—Titus
		Christian—James 1

Sharpening the Focus of the Church presents an overall perspective for Church Renewal. All of these books are available from your bookstore.

1
James Who?

James, a servant of God and of the Lord Jesus Christ (James 1:1).

This is a study in the book of James. But, as with any great piece of literature, you cannot understand the message of the book without knowing about the author. Who was James?

In many New Testament documents we can easily determine the author by autobiographical references in the books themselves. This was particularly true of Paul's New Testament letters. They were very personal epistles, either directed to churches he established on his missionary journeys or to individuals who were his fellow missionaries.

But we cannot say the same about the book of James.

First, it is not directed to a particular church or to an individual. In that sense it is not an ordinary epistle. Rather it is directed "to the twelve tribes scattered among the nations" (Jas. 1:1). Second, James says nothing specific about himself in this treatise, except simply in identifying himself as "James, a servant of God and of the Lord Jesus Christ" (1:1).

Though there are several prominent men in the New Testament who are called *James,* it is possible to identify the author of this book with a great degree of certainty. Fortunately, there are some very specific references to his family, his life, and his ministry in other parts of the New Testament. And once we identify *who* he is we can also understand more clearly why he wrote this book.

JAMES—HIS CHRISTIAN CONVERSION
(Acts 1:12-14)

Frequently the book of Acts provides a historical context for helping us to understand the New Testament. This is especially true of letters and other documents that were written to help Christians mature and grow in their Christian lives. As we might expect, this is also true of the book of James.

The first passage in Acts describes an event on the day of Pentecost. Christ had just returned to heaven from the Mount of Olives. The apostles, some of the women, and Jesus' brothers were gathered in an upper room in Jerusalem devoting themselves to prayer. In that room we can positively identify at least three men, perhaps four, who were named James.

The Son of Zebedee

First, there was James, one of the twelve apostles, and the older brother of John. James and John were the sons of Zebedee (Matt. 4:21; Mark 1:19; Luke 5:10). And they, along with Peter, were part of the inner circle among the twelve apostles. They had the unique privilege of being with Christ when He ascended a mountain and was transfigured before their very eyes (Matt. 17; Mark 9; Luke 9:28). They were also with Jesus when He raised Jairus's daughter from the dead (Mark 5:37; Luke 8:51). And they were particularly privileged to be with Christ as He prayed in the Garden of Gethsemane just before He was taken captive (Mark 14:33; Matt. 26:37).

This James was also the first of the apostles to give his life for Christ. Very early in the history of the church, before any of the New Testament books were written, he suffered martyrdom. King Herod ordered him executed (Acts 12:2). Consequently, this man could not be the author of the book of James.

The Son of Alphaeus

James, the son of Alphaeus, was also one of the twelve apostles who was in the upper room (Acts 1:13). On occasions he was called "James the younger" (Mark 15:40), perhaps because he was younger than James, the son of Zebedee. Most Bible interpreters do not believe this man wrote the book of James.

The Father of Judas

There's a third man named James who is also mentioned in Luke's historical account. He was the father of the apostle named Judas, the man, of course, who had *not* betrayed the Lord (Acts 1:13). There is no historical evidence that this James wrote *any* of the books in the New Testament.

The Son of Joseph

There was, however, another man present in the upper room also named James. However, he is not identified by name. Rather, he is included as one of the "brothers" of Jesus (Acts 1:14). Joseph, of course, would be his father and Mary his mother. And most biblical interpreters agree that this is the James who wrote the New Testament book we're about to study.

There was a time when James was very critical of Jesus. When his brother's popularity began to grow because of His healing and teaching ministry, James, along with his other brothers and sisters, were convinced that Jesus was "out of his mind" (Mark 3:21). To put it in twentieth-century terms, they thought He was going crazy. Later when Jesus claimed to be the Son of God, James, along with his brothers, "did not believe in him" (John 7:5). They joined their fellow Jews in denying that their brother was the Messiah. When the other apostles were expressing their faith in Christ (John 6:68), James was rejecting the Lord.

But something happened! James changed. He had seen Jesus taken captive, unfairly tried and cruelly crucified. More important, he had witnessed Christ's resurrection. Paul informs us that Jesus first "appeared to Peter, and then to the Twelve" (1 Cor. 15:5). After that "he appeared to more than five hundred of the brothers at the same time" (1 Cor. 15:6). And then He made a personal appearance to His brother James (1 Cor. 15:7).

Imagine James's response. The man who had severely criticized Jesus, the man who called Him insane, and the man who had believed that his brother was a fraud now stood face to face with the resurrected Christ. If James's heart had not been changed before, it must have happened at that moment. No longer was Jesus just a brother, a member of his family. He was now his personal Lord and Saviour.

JAMES—HIS LEADERSHIP POSITION

In time James came to be closely identified with the

apostles. This was a rare privilege. There were the original twelve men whom Jesus had specifically chosen (Judas Iscariot was replaced by Matthias—Acts 1:23-26). Later, Paul, called in a dramatic way by the Lord to become a missionary to the Gentiles, became an apostle. When Paul wrote his letter to the Galatian Christians he identified "James, the Lord's brother"—with the apostle (Gal. 1:19). He had emerged as a strong New Testament leader and was particularly active in the Jerusalem church. In fact, some identify James as the pastor or primary leader of this large and growing body of believers.

The apostle Peter also recognized James's position and authority in the church in Jerusalem. After James, John's brother, was martyred by Herod, Peter was also imprisoned and was scheduled for public trial. But God miraculously delivered him from prison. While he was sleeping between two soldiers, suddenly the chains binding him fell from Peter's wrists and he was led by an angel out of prison and into the streets. He made his way to a home where a group of Christians were praying for him. After telling the story of his dramatic deliverance, he instructed these Christians to be sure to share this information with "James" (Acts 12:17), who was no doubt James, the Lord's brother. This is significant, for it indicates that this man was already recognized as an important leader in the Jerusalem church.

JAMES—HIS THEOLOGICAL TRANSITION

For some time, even after Christ's return to heaven, the apostles did not understand God's salvation plan for all people. They continued to believe that only Jews could be saved. This is best exemplified in the life of Peter. Though a primary spokesman for Christianity, both on the day of Pentecost and after, he did not understand that Gentiles

could be saved. In fact, he did not come to this understanding until he saw Cornelius and his household respond
to the gospel. He then testified, "I *now* realize how true it
is that God does not show favoritism but accepts men from
every nation who fear him and do what is right" (Acts
10:34).[1]

It should not surprise us that James, the Lord's
brother, went through the same theological transition. The
historical context for his enlightenment was just as dramatic as Peter's was. It involved a very strategic and
tense conference in Jerusalem.

Several Jewish men had left Judea and had gone to
Antioch and there began teaching that Gentile Christians
had to be circumcised according to the Law of Moses in
order to be saved. Paul and Barnabas openly and publicly
confronted this issue, but could not solve the problem.
Consequently, they and other appointed leaders were
charged with the responsibility of going to Jerusalem to
"see the apostles and elders" about this theological matter
(Acts 15:1-2).

In the context of an intense discussion and interaction,
Peter shared how Cornelius became a Christian and how
this experience convinced him that Gentiles *can* be
saved—and by faith alone (Acts 15:6-9).

Paul and Barnabas also testified to this reality, and
after they finished speaking, James the Lord's brother
spoke up. He quoted the Old Testament to support what
Peter and Paul and Barnabas had been sharing. He sug-
gested that they not burden the Gentile converts with the
ceremonial aspects of the Law of Moses. He then pro-
posed some basic guidelines to keep these new believers
from becoming a stumbling block to their brothers in
Christ who were Jews. Furthermore, he specified that a
Christian should be morally pure in every respect (Acts
15:13-20).

This was a significant point in the life of the church and in James's life as well. For the church at large it meant they now understood that Jesus Christ came to die for the whole world, not just for Jews. And for James this new perspective affected his philosophy of ministry and leadership. From this point forward it was his desire to integrate what he had learned as a Jew with what he was learning about God's great plan of salvation for all mankind.

JAMES—HIS PASTORAL PROBLEMS

James's ministry continued to be primarily with Jewish Christians as he gave pastoral leadership to the Jerusalem church. This was probably one of the toughest leadership assignments given any man in the New Testament world. For one thing, many of the mature converts to Christ had left Jerusalem because of the initial persecution in the early days of the church (Acts 8:1). Though some of these people no doubt returned to their homes after the persecution subsided, many probably settled elsewhere. But the church continued to grow, and as it did it attracted many Jews who continued to be very zealous for the Law of Moses, even though they believed in Jesus Christ.

Predictably, this influx of Jews who continued to propagate the legalistic system they had been taught caused unusual problems in the church. Years later, when Paul returned to Jerusalem, he faced a church composed of thousands of people who were extremely hostile against anyone who would openly teach that salvation was by faith alone.

At this point in time, James was still the primary leader of the church, but he faced some very difficult challenges. He and all the elders welcomed Paul. They praised God when they heard about what was happening among the Gentiles. But, "they said to Paul: 'You see, brother, how many thousands of Jews have believed, and all of them are zealous for the law. They have been informed that you teach all the Jews who live among the Gentiles to turn away from Moses, telling them not to circumcise their children or live according to our customs" (Acts 21:20-21).

The frustration of James and all the elders is focused clearly with their next question: "What shall we do?" (Acts 21:22). And it is this overall historical context that will help us to understand more fully the letter that James wrote.

A LESSON IN HUMILITY

What we've just learned is more than some dramatic facts about a man who once was against Jesus and then turned to Him and became His follower. It is the story of a man who, though he became a great leader, continued to be a man of great humility.

This twentieth-century lesson may seem strange in view of all that could be said. But it stands out boldly when we look at the introduction to the book James wrote. He simply stated, "James, a servant of God and of the Lord Jesus Christ."

Had I been James I would have been tempted to introduce the letter with a few more words. It probably would have read, "James, a brother of Jesus Christ, who grew up with this Man, who observed His life, His miracles, and who heard Him teach; James, a man whom Jesus chose to visit personally after His resurrection; James, a man who was with the apostles when the Holy Spirit came; James, a man who later was closely identified with the apostles by the great apostle Paul; James, who eventually became the pastor of the largest church in the world."

In view of what James *could* have said, isn't it interesting that he only began his letter with the simple words, "James, a servant of God and of the Lord Jesus Christ"?

Stating our credentials is not wrong. In fact, Paul often had to in order to prove his apostleship, although on occasions it embarrassed him (2 Cor. 11:16-33). And so today it is not inappropriate in certain instances to present our qualifications and accomplishments; in fact, it is absolutely necessary in order to function in our culture.

An Unfortunate Trend

There is a trend today among Christians that is in many respects an overreaction. Many Christians were taught for so long that they were "nothing" that they downgraded their abilities, their talents, and their capabilities. A good self-image was falsely equated with spiritual pride. Counselors in particular, saw the negative results and emotional scars that were resulting from this unfortunate emphasis.

But even more unfortunate, many Christian counselors and leaders led people to overreact to this extreme point of view and current humanistic trends in the field of psychology and sociology continue to accentuate this overreaction. The feminist movement also added fuel to the fire. Today we're living in an era of "me-ism." Magazines and books roll off the presses promoting the idea that *"I am important and if I don't look out for myself, nobody will."*

And so today, even among Christians, we are moving into an era of self-promotion. This emphasis has spread quickly into the area of Christian leadership. And so among pastors, missionaries, evangelists and musicians, and other public figures, we see the emergence of self-styled Christian superstars.

Elaine and I had the privilege of attending the Gaither Praise Gathering several years in succession where I was given the opportunity to conduct several seminars. Participating in the program were a number of other seminar leaders and well-known musicians. I was greatly impressed with something Bill Gaither shared with all of us in a special session he had with all the program personnel prior to the beginning of the main conference sessions. "As we gather together," he said, "our major purpose is to honor and glorify Jesus Christ—not ourselves. There is no room in this gathering for superstars."

With that statement, Bill was emphasizing how easy it is to upstage another performer or speaker when we participate with others. What he was saying is true. It *is* easy to compete in ways that build ourselves up while putting others down. The Bible teaches that we're all to be servants of Jesus Christ, not ourselves. And if we're spiritual leaders it is especially important to be simply instruments that God can use to glorify Himself.

This does not mean a Christian should hide in a corner or refuse to use the talents God has given him lest he be lifted up with pride. It does not mean we should say no to unique opportunities for service that give us public visibility. It does not mean we should reject compliments as if we're not worthy to hear or accept them. And it doesn't mean we should hold back because others are threatened by us. But it *does* mean always putting Jesus Christ first and always being a servant to Him and to each other.

A Twentieth-Century James

I remember a man who was a great model to me. I have mentioned him before in my messages and books. His name was Harold Garner, a former professor of mine at Moody Bible Institute. He's now with the Lord, but I'll never forget something he shared with me. One statement is as fresh in my mind as if he stated it yesterday. During a time of prayer we had together he asked me to pray that he would never become "professional" in his ministry to others.

This man certainly did not mean that he didn't want to do things well. He did not mean that he wanted to be less than professional in dealing with others—as we use that term today. What he did mean was that he wanted to become a man who conducted his personal and platform ministry with warmth and deep concern for people. Furthermore, he was saying that he always wanted to sense that it was a privilege to have people come and listen to him speak or to seek him out for counsel. He was also saying that he did not want to evaluate his speaking opportunities by the number of people who would be there. I personally think that James would have been proud of my friend.

SOME GUIDELINES FOR MAINTAINING BALANCE
1. Be faithful in "little things."
2. When given a job, do it well, with all your heart, and without *expecting* public recognition; but when you get it, accept it gratefully. Be encouraged.
3. Let others promote your capabilities and accomplishments.
4. Demonstrate your capabilities by your "work" rather than your "words."
5. Honor others above yourself.
6. Don't put yourself down but don't be a self-promoter.
7. When you do get opportunities for public visibility, thank God for the opportunity; do your best but honor God.
8. Be on guard against extreme attitudes and actions.
Note: Insecurity is often the root of self-promotion.

A FINAL THOUGHT
James was a man who *was* prominent. He had a very important position. He was even a brother of the Lord Jesus Christ, growing up in the same home; but he did not have to talk about his family history, his position and accomplishments to prove to others who he was. His faithfulness in God's work was enough to let others know who

he was and that he was worth listening to. It appears that everyone who read this document would know who he was because he said simply, "James, a servant of God, and of the Lord Jesus Christ."

Note
1. Hereafter all italicized words in Scripture quotations are added by the author for emphasis.

2
Is There Really Power in Positive Thinking?

Consider it pure joy, my brothers, whenever you face trials of many kinds, because you know that the testing of your faith develops perseverance. Perseverance must finish its work so that you may be mature and complete, not lacking anything (James 1:2-4).

A number of years ago a book appeared on the scene written by a well-known minister, Norman Vincent Peale, entitled *The Power of Positive Thinking.* More recently another minister has picked up the theme in his own books. The idea that permeates Robert Schuller's philosophy of life and his sermons is "possibility thinking." And, of course, the business world is filled with men and women who have developed this theme in seminars designed to encourage and motivate people to think positively and succeed in the process. In fact, I was with a group of people recently who would not use the word *problems*. Rather, they were *challenges*. Interestingly, some of the most prominent leaders in this arena were evangelical Christians.

This leads us to consider the question which is the title of this chapter. "Is there *really* power in positive thinking?" James helps us answer that question from God's perspective. But first, let's set the stage!

JAMES'S AUDIENCE

James directed his thoughts "to the twelve tribes scattered among the nations" (Jas. 1:1). In this sense, it is not like a typical New Testament letter, particularly those that are written by Paul to individual churches (such as the Thessalonians, the Corinthians, the Colossians, etc.), or to individual church leaders (such as Timothy or Titus).

The audience James had in mind seems distinctively Jewish, though some Bible interpreters believe that the "twelve tribes" referred to in James's introduction include both Jews and Gentiles who responded to the gospel. It seems more reasonable, however, to take a literal approach to James's statement and conclude that he was indeed writing to *Jewish* Christians—God's chosen people who were, in Old Testament days, scattered throughout the world because of their rebellion and sin against God (Deut. 28:64). However, the people James was writing to were now Christians, those Jews who had accepted and believed in Jesus Christ as their promised Messiah. Furthermore, if the author *was* James the Lord's brother (as we believe he was), then the concerns expressed in this document relate in a special way to the problems James faced as a primary spiritual leader in the church in Jerusalem.

On the other hand, what James wrote to Jewish believers 2,000 years ago is intensely practical and relevant to *all* believers today. This is the miracle of God's written revelation. Paul wrote to Timothy—"*All* Scripture is God-breathed and is useful for teaching, rebuking, correcting and training in righteousness, so that the man of God may be thoroughly equipped for every good work" (2 Tim. 3:16-17). And this statement certainly includes the book of James.

Strange as it may seem, James exhorted his readers to "Consider it pure joy . . . whenever" they faced "trials of many kinds" (Jas. 1:2). In this statement, two ideas emerge that need explanation. The first is *joy* and the second is *trials*. Let's think about the second concept first.

"TRIALS OF MANY KINDS"
(James 1:2)

In the original language of the New Testament, the word translated "trials" is *peirasmos,* and is often translated "temptation." In fact, the King James reads, "My brethren, count it all joy when ye fall into divers *temptations.*" New Testament writers use the word *peirasmos* to refer to all kinds of difficulties that come into our lives. Some are directly related to Satan's efforts to lead us into sin, such as when Christ was tempted by Satan in the wilderness (Luke 4:13). Other instances involve things in our lives that may cause us to sin, such as riches (1 Tim. 6:9). There are also "trials" caused by those who hate Christ and consequently His followers as well. Those, too, are identified as *peirasmos* (1 Pet. 1:6; 4:12).

James wrote, "Consider it pure joy, my brothers, whenever you face trials of *many kinds.*" It seems he is referring not only to trials and difficulties we face because of circumstances beyond our control, but also to those temptations that come into our lives because of our own sinful desires and inclination. Both kinds of *peirasmos* interrelate, of course, because even circumstances beyond our control (such as persecution by non-Christians) can cause us to respond in sinful ways.

For example, what happens when someone mistreats you? If you're like me your natural response is to retaliate—to even the score! And yet, God makes it clear we are not to take vengeance on others—that is, to repay anyone evil for evil (Rom. 12:17; 1 Pet. 3:9).

Have you ever had a day when everything seems to go wrong? How do you respond to others—and to God? In these instances, frustration and anger are normal responses, and they are not necessarily sinful reactions. What we do with our anger, however, determines whether or not we submit to temptation and allow our reactions to become sinful (Eph. 4:26).

What *should* our attitude be when we "face trials of many kinds"? This leads us to the second concept we need to think about.

"CONSIDER IT PURE JOY"
(James 1:2)

How can we be joyful and glad when we face trials and temptations? Is it possible to experience positive emotions when Satan attacks us? When circumstances frustrate us? When people hurt us? When the things of the world ignite our carnal passions and desires?

First, we must understand that the biblical concept of joy—and particularly in this instance—is not synonymous with *pleasure*, such as we experience when we sit down to a delicious steak dinner, when we purchase a new car (and are able to pay cash), when we receive a raise, or ski down a beautiful mountain slope covered with several inches of newly-fallen snow. In fact, most of us do not have to *consider* these experiences "pure joy." They *are* pure joy.

The joy James is writing about involves the ability to look beyond the problem or difficulty we're experiencing and see the opportunity to become more like Jesus Christ. Furthermore, it means seeing how God can further His work through the problem we're encountering. Thus Paul could say, as he wrote to the Philippians from a Roman prison, "But what does it matter? The important thing is that in every way, whether from false motives or true, Christ is preached. And because of this I *rejoice*. Yes, and I will continue to *rejoice*" (Phil. 1:18).

Much of what we feel depends on our *attitude* towards the problem and on our subsequent *actions*. Negative feelings, of course, are natural and normal when we face painful situations. But if we can see beyond the immediate events, we are capable of eventually turning negatives into positives. This is particularly true when we think eternally, and see beyond our life on earth.

Even secular and non-Christian religious writers have discovered this to be true. The stoic philosopher, Seneca, once wrote, "True joy is an exacting business."[1] Rabbi R. Joshua B. Levi stated, "He who gladly accepts the suffering of this world brings salvation to the world."[2] And Mary Baker Eddy, the founder of a religious system known as Christian Science, taught her followers to deny the existence of matter, that there is no such thing as evil and sin, and that disease and death are an illusion. And it is not surprising that people who accept her teachings, and who do not accept these realities *as* realities, often experience some very unusual physiological and psychological benefits. In this sense, there *is* power in positive thinking.

Think for a moment! If non-Christians can view a personal difficulty with positive attitudes and actions, even denying that it exists, and consequently experience a degree of inner peace in the midst of the difficulty, think what *should* happen with the person who has a true Christian perspective on reality when trials and temptations come!

And this leads us to another question. What is a true Christian perspective? James proceeds to answer this question as well.

"THE TESTING OF YOUR FAITH DEVELOPS PERSEVERANCE"
(James 1:3)

Trials and temptations *do* exist. They *are* realities. As James Adamson states, *peirasmos* is "the great common experience of the Redeemer and the redeemed."[3] Jesus Christ Himself faced them all—including execution and death as an innocent man. And, as we read in the book of Hebrews, "Because he himself suffered when he was tempted, he is able to help those who are being tempted" (Heb. 2:18).

Christians, therefore, do not have to deny the existence of problems to face them with positive attitudes and actions. Thus James tells us to look beyond the trials to see what can happen in our lives because they *do* exist. He reminds us that we can face these problems both realistically and positively because we know that our faith is being tested, and when it is being tested, we develop *perseverance* (James 1:3).

The New Testament word for *perseverance* could be better translated "steadfastness." When a Christian faces trials and temptations, he has an opportunity to either give up in defeat, or to develop his capacity to endure and maintain steadfast commitment to do the will of God.

"Doing the will of God" is, of course, a key phrase. There are some Christians who are intensely steadfast for the wrong reasons. For example, I may refuse to give in or give up in a certain set of circumstances because I'm just plain stubborn. The basis of my motivation may be arrogance, pride, ego and self-protection. I'm not really concerned about the will of God for myself or for others. In these instances I'm steadfast because of my own self-will, not God's will. In fact, most examples of steadfastness in today's world probably illustrate this kind of self-centered perseverance.

Biblical and spiritual steadfastness is quite another matter. The decision to endure is based on the desire to do the will of God, no matter what the cost personally. This kind of endurance is beautifully illustrated and contrasted in the award-winning film *Chariots of Fire*. Two runners were training for the 1924 Olympics. One, a Christian, was committed to winning because of the abilities that God gave him. He wanted to honor God with his endurance and steadfastness. This does not mean he did not gain personal satisfaction from running and winning, but his overriding motivation was to glorify God. To that end he trained well and with determination.

Another young man was determined to win because of pride and sheer ego. He was willing to go to almost any lengths to achieve his goal. Any kind of defeat, even while training, brought intense depression and humiliation.

As it turned out, both men won! One proved his own abilities and what can be achieved by steadfastness that focuses on oneself. The other won to use his abilities to honor God.

How can we be sure of what really motivated these men? There's another dimension to the story that helps us answer this question. The Christian had deep convictions about competing on the Lord's day. Since the 100-meter race he had trained for was scheduled on Sunday, he refused to run. No matter what the pressure from the Olympic committee or the ridicule from the press, or the cost to him personally, he was willing to pay the price because of his spiritual convictions.

As it turned out, he was allowed to run on another day, but in a more difficult race than he had trained for. Rather than competing in the 100-meter race, he entered the 400-meter. He set a new Olympic record! Whether or not you agree with Eric Liddel's specific interpretation of God's will regarding the Lord's day, we must admire his commitment to high principles, and moreso his desire to obey God no matter what the cost. He steadfastly refused to violate his principles, even if it meant giving up his dream of winning an Olympic medal.

Spiritual steadfastness then is a biblical goal in itself. It is developed as we face trials and temptations victoriously, choosing to do the will of God no matter what the cost to us personally. This is probably best illustrated in Scripture by Moses, who, "when he had grown up, refused to be known as the son of Pharaoh's daughter. He chose to be mistreated along with the people of God rather than to enjoy the pleasures of sin for a short time." Furthermore, "he regarded disgrace for the sake of Christ as of greater value than the treasures of Egypt, because he was looking ahead to his reward. By faith he left Egypt, not fearing the king's anger." Moses *"persevered* because he saw him who is invisible" (Heb. 11:24-27).

"PERSEVERANCE MUST FINISH ITS WORK SO THAT YOU MAY BE MATURE AND COMPLETE" (James 1:4)

Steadfastness is more than a goal in itself. It is also a means to an even greater goal—maturity in Christ. Thus James wrote that "perseverance must finish its work so that you may be mature and complete, not lacking anything" (Jas. 1:4). As we face trials victoriously, as we steadfastly refuse to give in to temptations that plague our souls, we will become more and more like Jesus Christ. And then someday—but not until then—we will be transformed totally into His image. At that time we will hear from His lips, "Well done, thou good and faithful servant."

A PERSONAL RESPONSE

First, isolate the difficulty: What major trial or temptation are you facing?

A financial crisis	Unjust criticism	Overeating
A physical problem	Bitterness	A family problem
Depression	Alcohol	A materialistic attitude
A marital problem	Jealousy	A natural disaster
Greed	A business problem	A social misunderstanding
Sexual temptation	Persecution	A neighborhood conflict

Other _____

Second, discover God's perspective: What does God say in His Word regarding what your specific attitudes and actions should be regarding this problem?

Example: If you are being "unjustly criticized," the Bible says you should not retaliate.

Note: This does not mean you do not have the right to defend yourself, but you should not take vengeance. There is a difference. In your situation, what should your response be?

Third, begin to think positively about the problem: A personalized paraphrase of James 1:2-4:

I will look at this problem as an opportunity to become more mature and complete in Christ. I will see it as an opportunity to develop my ability to be steadfast in doing what *God* says rather than what *I* want to do. I will not allow this problem to overpower me or defeat me and keep me from developing in my Christian life. I will look at this problem as an opportunity to prove to myself and others that I am indeed a born-again believer. I will look forward to that day when I'm with Christ, joyfully entering into that experience because I have lived for Christ rather than myself. Above all else, I will obey God because I love Him more than I love myself.

A FINAL THOUGHT

"No temptation has seized you except what is common to man. And God is faithful; he will not let you be tempted beyond what you can bear. But when you are tempted, he will also provide a way out so that you can stand up under it" (1 Cor. 10:13).

Notes
1. James Adamson, *The International Commentary on the New Testament: The Epistle of James* (Grand Rapids: Wm. B. Eerdmans Publishing Company, 1975), p. 53.
2. *Ibid.*, p. 53.
3. *Ibid.*, p. 52.

3
Who Is Wise and Understanding Among You?

If any of you lacks wisdom, he should ask God, who gives generously to all without finding fault, and it will be given to him. But when he asks, he must believe and not doubt, because he who doubts is like a wave of the sea, blown and tossed by the wind. That man should not think he will receive anything from the Lord; he is a double-minded man, unstable in all he does (James 1:5-8).

To understand this passage of Scripture we must understand the larger context. There is continuity between what James states in verses 2-4 and here in verses 5-8. Let's establish that continuity.

James begins his letter by exhorting his readers to look

at trials and temptations with a positive attitude, seeing in those difficulties an opportunity to put their faith to the test, consequently developing perseverance and steadfastness in their Christian lives. This, James continues, will lead to more and more maturity. To put it more specifically, he states that when experiences of being steadfast in the midst of trials finishes its work, we will be "mature and complete, not *lacking anything*" (Jas. 1:4). But James says—and here is the point of continuity, "If any of you *lacks wisdom,* he should ask God, who gives generously to all without finding fault, and it will be given to him" (Jas. 1:5).

There is a direct correlation in James's teaching between "being mature and complete" and having "wisdom." Becoming wise is part of the process of becoming mature in Christ. If we lack wisdom we are not as "mature and complete" as we can be.

There is another connection. To face trials and temptations victoriously (that is, with steadfastness and perseverance) we must have wisdom, no matter where we are in the process of Christian growth. There is no way we can stand fast in doing the will of God in the midst of difficulties and problems without it. In fact, without the wisdom James is talking about we'll have difficulty even knowing what God's will is!

WHAT IS WISDOM?

This leads us to a very basic question. What does the word *wisdom* actually mean? As usual, the Bible itself is its own best interpreter. The Greek word is *sophia,* and means "broad and full intelligence," namely, *full knowledge.* In fact, it is frequently used in conjunction with the word *knowledge* in the context of prayer, spiritual growth, and being steadfast and mature in living the Christian life.

Paul's Three Prayers

Paul illustrates what James is talking about very graphically in his prayers for various Christians. Note the following prayers and how what he prays for *does* relate to what James exhorts us to do.

Writing to the Ephesians he said: "I keep asking that the God of our Lord Jesus Christ, the glorious Father, may give you the spirit of *wisdom* and *revelation,* so that you may know him better. I pray also that the *eyes of your heart* may be enlightened in order that you may know the *hope* to which he has called you, the riches of his glorious inheritance in the saints, and his incomparably great power for us who believe" (Eph. 1:17-19).

In this passage there is a direct connection between Paul's prayer that the Ephesians might have *wisdom* and that they might "know the *hope*" to which God had called them. That hope certainly involves their eternal salvation.

The correlation with James's exhortation to be steadfast in the midst of trials and difficulties is obvious. Without this kind of hope there would be no motivation to persevere and be steadfast.

Paul's prayer for the Colossians is even more specific: "We have not stopped praying for you and asking God to fill you with the *knowledge* of his will through all spiritual *wisdom* and *understanding.* And we pray this in order that you may live a life worthy of the Lord and may please him in every way: bearing fruit in every good work, growing in the knowledge of God, being strengthened with all power according to his glorious might so that you may have *great endurance* and *patience,* and *joyfully* giving thanks to the Father" (Col. 1:9-12).

In this prayer Paul actually uses the same words as James. "Wisdom" and "understanding" results in "great *endurance*" and "patience," and enables us to face difficult circumstances "joyfully." Thus James wrote, "Consider it pure joy . . . whenever you face trials of any kind."

Paul's most succinct prayer illustrating what James is saying is found in Philippians: "And this is my prayer: that your love may abound more and more in *knowledge* and *depth of insight,* so that you may be *able to discern what is best* and may be *pure* and *blameless* until the day of Christ, filled with the *fruit of righteousness* that comes through Jesus Christ—to the glory and praise of God" (Phil. 1:9-11).

Here Paul defines wisdom more functionally as "depth of insight" and being able "to discern what is best."

An Old Testament Illustration

There is a direct correlation between what Solomon experienced and what God wants for every Christian. After Solomon was appointed King of Israel, the Lord appeared to him in a dream and said, "Ask for whatever you want me to give you." Rather than asking for wealth, health, and victory over his enemies, Solomon said, "I am only a little child and do not know how to carry out my duties . . . . So give your servant a *discerning heart* to govern your people and to *distinguish between right and wrong*" (1 Kings 3:5,7-9).

We read that "the Lord was pleased" with Solomon's request for wisdom. "I will do what you have asked," the Lord responded. "I will give you a *wise* and *discerning heart*" (vv. 10,12).

There is one thing that is clear from Scripture: God *is always* pleased when we ask for wisdom to do His will. He *wants* to answer this kind of prayer.

Immediately after this event, the author of 1 Kings records for us an experience Solomon had that illustrates how he used the wisdom God gave him. "Two prostitutes came to the king and stood before him." These two women lived together. Both of them gave birth to children. One night one of the women lost her son. "She got up in the middle of the night," removed the living child from his mother's bed and put the dead child in his place. In the morning, the woman whose child was still alive awakened but found the dead child. When she looked carefully she noticed it wasn't her son. But the woman who had done this thing denied it. She claimed that the living child was her own.

Both of these women came before the king. After listening to the story, Solomon asked his attendants to bring him a sword so that he might "cut the living child in two and give half to one and half to the other."

What happened, of course, was just what Solomon anticipated would happen. The mother who was the real mother came to the child's rescue. She voluntarily asked that the king give the child to the other woman. The one who was *not* the real mother agreed with the king's order.

Solomon discerned what had happened. "Give the living baby to the first woman," he ordered. "Do not kill him; *she is his mother.*"

Solomon's fame spread throughout the kingdom. We read that "when all Israel heard the verdict the king had given, they held the king in awe, because they saw that he had *wisdom from God* to administer justice" (1 Kings 3:16-28).

Reviewing this story reminds me of another story. There was another king who had lost the respect of his people. One day he was reminded of Solomon's experience. He reviewed this Old Testament story and was greatly impressed. "If only I could have that kind of opportunity," he thought to himself, "then I would regain the respect of *my* people."

Several days later—would you believe—two women appeared before him with the same problem. "Wonderful," he thought to himself. "Now is my opportunity to demonstrate my wisdom just as Solomon did!"

After hearing the story and the argument between the two women, he asked his six-foot-four armed attendant who was standing beside his throne to give him a sword.

"What are you going to do, sir?" asked the big soldier.

"I'm going to cut the child in two," the king responded.

"Oh, sir, you can't do that!" protested his armed guard.

Pointing his finger directly at the man, the king quickly retorted, "That proves it! You're the mother!"

We laugh at this ridiculous story. But in many respects it illustrates for us the difference between *knowing* certain things and being able to *apply* that knowledge in wise ways. Godly wisdom enables us to apply knowledge in the midst of all kinds of circumstances and situations—including trials and tribulations.

HOW DO WE RECOGNIZE WISDOM?

James himself tells us later in his book how we can recognize wisdom. "Who is wise and understanding among you?" he wrote. "Let him show it by his good life, by deeds done in the *humility* that comes from wisdom" (Jas. 3:13).

The wisdom that James is talking about here is wisdom that comes from God. There is, however, another kind of wisdom—wisdom that "does not come down from heaven, but is earthly, unspiritual, of the devil" (3:15). That kind of wisdom, James says, reflects bitter "envy and selfish ambition." The result is "disorder and ever evil practice." By contrast, "the wisdom that comes from heaven is first of all *pure;* then *peace loving, considerate, submissive, full of mercy* and *good fruit, impartial* and *sincere*" (James 1:16-17).

There are, then, two kinds of wisdom. In addition to godly wisdom there is the "wisdom of this world" that also enables people to apply what they know. However, it is sinful and evil and it, too, comes from the heart. Furthermore, the world today is filled with people who have worldly wisdom—college professors, scientists, economists, government leaders, writers, film producers, etc. Some of the most brilliant people today are operating with worldly wisdom.

The wisdom that God gives to Christians to enable them to live according to His will also comes from the heart. But this wisdom reflects God's character. This kind of life-style is particularly outlined in Paul's prayer for the Philippians. Thus he prays that they might have wisdom that gives them "depth of insight" to "be able to *discern* what is best" so that they "may be *pure* and *blameless*" and "filled with the *fruit of righteousness*" (Phil. 1:9-11).

HOW DO WE RECEIVE GOD'S WISDOM?

The Means—"Prayer"

James tells us specifically how we can receive wisdom, and, as we see, both Paul and Solomon illustrate it—we ask God for it. And, continues James, God will give it "generously to all *without finding fault."* That is, the Lord will not hold our past failures and sins against us. If our hearts are right towards Him, He will hear us.

Have you ever been afraid to approach someone to ask for something because of something that has happened in the past? You know full well that you did something wrong and, even though you've asked forgiveness of that person, you know you've never received it. And you know that it will be held against you for the rest of your life.

Not so with God. We've all sinned against Him. But in Christ He has forgiven us. Our sins are buried in the depths of the sea. He will not remind us of our sins or withhold wisdom from us because of our past failures.

The Condition—"Unwavering Faith"

But there is a condition for receiving God's wisdom through prayer. James outlines it clearly. When we ask, we "must believe and not doubt."

James then uses an illustration to get a point across. "He who doubts is like a wave of the sea, blown and tossed by the wind." Consequently, James continues, "That man should not think he will receive anything from the Lord; he is a double-minded man, unstable in all he does."

This nautical illustration, which probably comes from James's experience with the Sea of Galilee, helps us understand what he means by faith and the *opposite* of faith—which is doubt. Storms arise quickly on the Sea of Galilee. Some are so severe that most small craft cannot survive the pounding waves. It is nigh to impossible to steer a steady course.

A person "who doubts" wrote James, "is like a wave of the sea, blown and tossed by the wind." Leaving the analogy, he then becomes very specific in describing the kind of doubt he has in mind. He describes it as being "double-minded." This kind of person is "unstable in all he does." Bunyan, in his classic allegory *Pilgrim's Progress,* calls this kind of Christian "Mr. Look-Both-Ways."

The overall picture of the "doubter" portrayed by James is a person who is undecided as to whether or not he wants to follow Jesus Christ. In that sense he is dealing with a Christian who wants help from God but only when he feels he absolutely needs it. When things are going well for him he follows the wisdom of the world. His life is conformed to the world's system. But in a crisis when he is unable to handle the situation on his own, he turns to God.

Though it is true that God is forgiving and does not hold our past sins against us, He also knows when we are trying to manipulate Him for our own selfish ends. Thus James wrote later, "When you ask, you do not receive, because you ask with *wrong motives*" (4:3).

Doubt, then, is more than momentary weakness. It reflects a life-style of wavering between following after God or following after the world. It reflects a person who is "unstable in *all* he does."

What then is faith? It is best illustrated by the man who came to Jesus to ask Him to heal his son who had been plagued with convulsions since childhood. "Everything is possible," Jesus responded, "for him who believes." His response was one that, if we're honest, we will all have to acknowledge. "I do believe," he said. "Help me overcome my unbelief." Jesus then healed the boy. (See Mark 9:14-24.)

In our minds there will always be an element of unbelief, no matter how committed we are to Jesus Christ. We certainly waver. But this is much different from being "double-minded." God honors what faith we have. Though we may stumble and fall, and though we fail on occasion, God hears and responds to our cries for help. He understands our hearts.

I was talking recently with someone who was feeling angry towards God and consequently feeling very guilty. In his heart he really didn't want to feel that way. He didn't want to be angry.

My response was that in this situation God understands that anger and sees beyond those surface feelings. He looks deep into the heart, and in that person's heart is a desire to conform his life to Jesus Christ. This reality is dramatically illustrated in the life of David, king of Israel. Though he seriously failed God on several occasions, God had mercy on him because He knew the deep desires of his heart. In fact, the Bible describes David as a "man after God's own heart."

This description in no way excuses David's failures. He suffered deeply as he faced the lingering consequences of his sin. But David was in no way a "double-minded man." Deep down in his heart he wanted to do the will of God.

WHAT IS THE PROCESS GOD USES TO GIVE WISDOM?

1. *God Gives Wisdom Directly in Answer to Prayer.*

James makes this point clear. If we lack wisdom, we should ask God. However, there are at least two cautions. First, James is *not* speaking of receiving revealed *Truth* as was given to those who authored the Scriptures (John 14:26; 16:13). To misunderstand this point can lead to some serious problems. In fact, this is one reason why books are written that are considered to be on par with the Scriptures. The result is usually doctrinal error.

Secondly, James is not speaking of the "gift" of wisdom mentioned in 1 Corinthians 12:8. James makes it clear that *every* Christian can have wisdom through prayer, whereas the *gift* of wisdom was given to *some* in the body of Christ, not all (1 Cor. 12:8).

2. *God Gives Wisdom Through the Scriptures.*

God's truth in the Bible *is* wisdom. And since the Word of God is revealed Truth, it is the most important wisdom a Christian can obtain. This is why it is so important that we study the Scriptures on a regular basis.

3. *God Gives Wisdom Through Other Mature Christians.*

No Christian can grow and mature in isolation from other Christians. We need one another. Therefore, the body of Christ provides a primary source for discovering wisdom. This is particularly true of men and women who are mature and experienced in their Christian lives. And this leads to another way in which God gives wisdom.

4. *God Gives Wisdom Through Experience.*

Someone has said that "A man begins cutting his wisdom teeth the first time he bites off more than he can chew." Though humorous, this statement in itself contains wisdom. I look back on my own life and have to conclude that some of my greatest learning experiences have come through difficulties. It's at times like this that God really gets our attention. And sometimes our greatest lessons in wisdom come through failure. Unfortunately, some of us do not learn from these experiences. However, we can— and if we do, it is one of the greatest sources of wisdom. Furthermore, when we see a difficult situation as an opportunity to learn, it makes the experience even more tolerable.

A PERSONALIZED PRAYER

Father, I come to you, first of all committing my life to you. I will follow you and your will for me, not the ways of Satan and this world. I relinquish my "doublemindedness" and ask you to help me move in your direction with singleness of heart and purpose.

I now ask you to give me your wisdom to _____
_____
_____

Please give me that wisdom so that I might honor you in all that I do. I'm waiting expectantly for your answer— though it be directly by giving me insight and discernment; though it be through the Scriptures; though it be through other Christians who are more wise than I in facing this situation; or though it be through experience that will teach me that wisdom.

Father, I believe you are interested in me and my concerns. I believe you are going to answer my prayer. I acknowledge my weakness, but as the man of old who came to you on behalf of his ill son, "I do believe; *help me overcome my unbelief.*"

Thank you for hearing my prayer. I'm waiting expectantly for your answer.

In Jesus' name, Amen.

4
What Is Your Life?

*The brother in humble circumstances ought to
take pride in his high position. But the one who is
rich should take pride in his low position, because
he will pass away like a wild flower. For the son
rises with a scorching heat and withers the plant;
its blossom falls and its beauty is destroyed. In
the same way, the rich man will fade away even
while he goes about his business.* (James 1:9-11).

Benjamin Franklin once wrote: "Money never made a
man happy yet, nor will it. There is nothing in its nature to
produce happiness. The more a man has, the more he
wants. Instead of its filling a vacuum, it makes one. If it
satisfies one want, it doubles and triples that want another
way."

John D. Rockefeller, Jr. wrote, "The poorest man I

know is the man who has nothing but money." And, the late Robert Horton said the greatest lesson he learned from his life was "that people who set their minds and hearts on money are equally disappointed whether they get it or whether they don't."

Having money or the lack of it has always been a problem in this world. Those who have lots of it consistently tell us it is *not* the basis of happiness or contentment. And, of course, they ought to know. On the other hand, those who have very little of this world's goods and possessions believe that if they could just discover the proverbial pot at the end of the rainbow they would have everything they need to be happy.

James dealt with this universal problem when he wrote to Christians in the New Testament world. And it is not without significance that he treats this subject immediately after he states what a Christian's perspective should be towards trials and temptations. "Consider it pure joy," he wrote, "whenever you face trials of many kinds." And he then dealt specifically with what causes every human being the greatest trials and temptations in this life— material possessions (Jas. 1:9-11). He spoke first to the Christians who had very little of this world's goods.

THE BROTHER IN HUMBLE CIRCUMSTANCES (James 1:9)

There have always been more poor people in this world than rich people. And the New Testament world had more than its share of those who were poor. It should not surprise us that the great majority of people who followed Jesus Christ and became Christians were poor. Those who had little of this world's goods were looking for a better life. And what Jesus taught about the abundant life He would give them certainly captured their attention (John 10:10).

Humble Circumstances

When these people became Christians they discovered rather quickly that following Jesus Christ did not automatically solve their economic problems. Those who became Christians in the midst of humble circumstances often remained in humble circumstances the rest of their lives. The facts are that the New Testament world, as is true in many places in the world today, had few opportunities to break loose from cultural circumstances and to create a better life financially.

This is difficult for those of us who are living in the free world, and particularly the United States of America, to understand. We are surrounded with opportunities. It is a part of our political and economic philosophy. Even in the midst of our inflationary trends there are still unique opportunities for people from all walks of life and from all kinds of economic backgrounds to better their economic situation. Where else could a man or woman with no inheritance, no lengthy credit references, no single financial backer, actually become a millionaire? It is possible in America, because it happens. And most of us know people who have achieved this status in life in a remarkably short period of time.

I'll never forget the first time the realization of our unique opportunities in America to better ourselves hit me with full force. My wife and I were visiting a foreign country. As we drove through the countryside we saw human conditions that literally made us sick to our stomachs. People lived in little shacks that most of us would not even allow farm animals to occupy. As we entered the outskirts of one large city we saw people living in caves.

But as we traveled on into the city where we stayed overnight we drove through a section that made the most affluent areas in American cities look second class. Beautiful three- and four-story mansions, constructed of pure marble, occupied whole city blocks. Limousines were parked in driveways that were nestled in beautiful, landscaped surroundings. Servants' quarters were more luxurious than many middle-class American homes.

While visiting this country we had all kinds of mixed emotions. We felt desperately sorry for the poor in that country, for it really dawned upon us for the first time that there are many people in this world who will never have the opportunity to break out of their economic circumstances in life. If they are born into these conditions, they will die in these conditions. And even if they could better themselves, most would never know about the possibility for they would never learn to read a newspaper or book, they would never see a television program and they would never hear a radio broadcast.

We also felt a sense of guilt because we had so much compared with those we saw who had literally nothing. But it was a false sense of guilt, for God does not want us to feel guilty simply because we have more than others. And we could do very little to alleviate the poverty in this city.

There was another benefit to this experience. It helped us to understand more clearly the conditions that existed in the New Testament world. People who were poor would most often remain poor, comparatively speaking, even if they became Christians. Their political and economic environment did not make allowances for self-improvement.

A High Position

There was one thing that *did* drastically change their perspective on life—their *eternal hope*. Thus James wrote, "The brother in *humble circumstances* ought to take pride in his *high position*." (Jas. 1:9).

"Humble circumstances" literally refers to *not* having

much of this world's goods. But James reminds them that in God's sight, what they have materially has nothing to do with their "high position" in Christ. THey may be poor by this world's standards, but exceedingly "rich" in God's sight. They were "heirs of God and co-heirs with Christ" (Rom. 8:17).

This truth was captured and expressed by the song-writer Harriett Buell, who wrote "The Child of a King":

> My Father is rich in houses and lands,
> He holdeth the wealth of the world in His hands!
> Of rubies and diamonds, of silver and gold,
> His coffers are full—He has riches untold.

> I'm a child of the King, a child of the King!
> With Jesus, my Savior, I'm a child of the King!

The practical implication of this truth, however, is expressed in the last two stanzas of this hymn.

> I once was an outcast, a stranger on earth,
> A sinner by choice and an alien by birth:
> But I've been adopted, my name's written down—
> An heir to a mansion, a robe, and a crown.

> A tent or a cottage, why should I care?
> They're building a palace for me over there!
> Though exiled from home, yet still I may sing:
> All glory to God, I'm a child of the King!

This is what James is referring to when he encouraged Christians in the New Testament world to "take pride" in their "high position." Though their worldly circumstances were very "humble" indeed, their heavenly circumstances were elegant. To quote Peter, they had "an inheritance" that would "never perish, spoil or fade—kept in heaven" (1 Pet. 1:4). Thus James was saying, Don't be ashamed! Hold your heads high! Don't be intimidated by those who have more than you do! In God's sight, you are equal, even with those Christians who have more of this world's goods than you do!

THE ONE WHO IS RICH
(James 1:10)

The next words are directed to affluent Christians: The "rich should take pride in his low position." On the surface these are rather strange words. But they are potent when we read on to discover what James actually meant.

What James Did Not Mean

Before we look at what James had in mind specifically, it's important to emphasize that he is *not* saying in this passage that it is wrong or sinful to *be* rich or *become* rich. The Bible is replete with examples of God's servants who were extremely well off materially.

• Abraham "had become *very wealthy* in livestock and in silver and gold" (Gen. 13:2).
• Abraham's son Isaac was likewise a very rich man. In fact, we read that Isaac's "wealth continued to grow until he became *very wealthy*" (Gen. 26:13).
• Isaac's son, Jacob, also "grew *exceedingly prosperous*" (Gen. 30:43).
• Years later, David "enjoyed long life, *wealth* and honor" (1 Chron. 29:28), and during his lifetime he was identified by the Lord Himself as a "man after his own heart" (1 Sam. 13:14).
• King Solomon, of course, surpassed his ancestors as

well as his contemporaries. We read that he "was *greater in riches* and wisdom than all the other kings of the earth" (2 Chron. 9:22).

As we move into the New Testament let's not forget:
• Joseph, "a *rich man* from Arimathea" who sought permission to remove the Lord's body from the cross and tenderly and lovingly placed Him in "his own new tomb that he had cut out of the rock" (Matt. 27:57,60).
• Barnabas, a wealthy "real estate man" in Jerusalem, who sold some of his holdings and used the money to help needy Christians (Acts 4:36-37).
• Philemon, Paul's wealthy friend who lived in Colosse; a man who evidently opened his home to Paul as he passed through on his missionary tours (Philemon 22).

The Bible not only includes numerous examples of many God-fearing people who were wealthy, but the Lord also makes it clear that He delights in blessing His children in a material way. His promises to Israel are clear-cut and to the point. If they obeyed Him, He promised to give them "the ability to produce wealth" (Deut. 8:18). Part of that obedience involved their tithes and offerings. In the book of Malachi, the last book of the Old Testament, we read that God told Israel to "bring the whole tithe (10 percent) into the storehouse ... Test me in this," God said, "and see if I will not throw open the floodgates of heaven and pour out so much blessing that you will not have room enough for it" (Mal. 3:10).

What James Does Mean

The Bible, then, does *not* teach that riches are wrong per se. But the Bible clearly warns that there are temptations and difficulties associated with riches. One of those problems is that people who are wealthy tend to rely on their material possessions for their security and happiness. Furthermore, they may tend to become materialistic in attitude and actions and want more and more, as Benjamin Franklin reminded us earlier. In addition, wealth can cause people to make decisions that often cause a great deal of heartache and difficulty, and in some instances, lead to sin.

Paul touched all of these issues and concerns when he wrote to Timothy, stating that "people who want to get rich fall into temptation and a trap and into many foolish and harmful desires that plunge men into ruin and destruction" (1 Tim. 6:9). The reason this happens, Paul continued, is that "the love of money is a root of all kinds of evil. Some people, eager for money, have wandered from the faith and pierced themselves with many griefs" (6:10).

Later in the same letter, Paul exhorted Timothy to "command those who are rich in this present world not to be *arrogant* nor to put their *hope* in wealth, which is so uncertain, but to put their hope in God, who richly provides us with everything for our enjoyment" (6:17).

Against this larger backdrop of Scripture, we can better understand James's statement to those Christians who were wealthy. Those who had little of this world's goods were "to take *pride*" in their "high position"—their position in Jesus Christ. "But the one who is rich," James wrote, "should take *pride* in his low position."

What does James mean by a rich man's "low position"? He is referring to the fact that material things, and particularly our life on this planet, are not enduring. The rich man himself "will pass away like a wild flower." James elaborates in the next verse when he wrote, "For the sun rises with scorching heat and withers the plant; its blossom falls and its beauty is destroyed. In the same way, the rich man will fade away even while he goes about his business" (Jas. 1:11).

History has verified this reality even in the lifetime of most of us. In 1923, a group of the world's most successful financiers met at the Edgewater Beach Hotel in Chicago. Collectively, these tycoons controlled more wealth than there was in the United States treasury, and for years newspapers and magazines had been printing their success stories and urging the youth of the nation to follow their example.

What had happened in the lives of these men just twenty-seven years later?

• Charles Schwab, the president of the largest independent steel company, lived on borrowed money the last five years of his life and died penniless.

• Arthur Cutten, the greatest wheat speculator, died abroad insolvent.

• Richard Whitney, the president of the New York Stock Exchange, was eventually released from Sing-Sing.

• Albert Fall, a member of the president's cabinet, was pardoned from prison so he could die at home.

• Jesse Livermore, the greatest bear in Wall Street, committed suicide.

• Leon Fraser, the president of the Bank of International Settlement, committed suicide.

• Ivar Krueger, the head of the world's greatest monopoly, committed suicide.

All of these men had learned how to make money, but not one of them had learned how to live. Their life stories underscore in a dramatic way that James was right. Just as a wild flower and the grass passes away, so "the rich man will fade away even while he goes about his business."

In the earlier passage in James dealing with wisdom, the author was his own best interpreter. Later on in his letter, he described and contrasted "heavenly wisdom" with "earthly wisdom." And the same is true of his statement about riches in verses 10 and 11. In chapter 4, he elaborates with a straightforward warning to those who are rich. "Now listen, you who say, 'Today or tomorrow we will go to this or that city, spend a year there, carry on business and make money.' Why, you do not even know what will happen tomorrow. *What is your life?* You are a mist that appears for a little while and then vanishes. Instead, you ought to say, 'If it is the Lord's will we will live and do this or that.' As it is, you *boast* and *brag*. All such *boasting* is evil" (Jas. 4:13-16).

Rich people should boast about their "low position" rather than their money and their ability to make more. Specifically, James is saying, Let people know your riches are not the most important thing in life—not just with words, but with your actions. Let people know that your eternal perspective is far more important than your earthly perspective. Let people see that you are not putting your trust in your wealth; that you know that you could pass out of this life any moment, but that your security is in Christ and in your hope of eternal life. Let people observe that you—to quote Jesus—are storing up "treasures in heaven" rather than "treasures on earth." Let people see that you are not a "double-minded" person, trying to serve two masters—"God and money" (Matt. 6:19-24). Let people experience the fact that you are seeking God's kingdom first and His righteousness (Matt. 6:33). Let people observe that you are taking seriously Paul's exhortation to Timothy to "command them [those who are rich] to do good, to be *rich in good deeds,* and to be *generous* and willing to share" (1 Tim. 6:18).

LESSONS FOR TWENTIETH-CENTURY CHRISTIANS

First, those of us who live in America must realize that most of us are not "poor" in the New Testament sense of that word. We may not be rich either, and we may not have much, but most of us can earn enough to meet our needs. Furthermore, we live in a culture that has given us unusual opportunities to better ourselves if we're indeed willing to do what is necessary to achieve that goal.

And this we should do and can do without violating God's principles. But we must do so with one objective in mind—to honor God and glorify Him in all that we do. And if God honors our efforts and blesses us with excess money, we must be on guard against the temptations we will inevitably face. We must be on guard against Satan's subtle traps. And as parents we must be doubly on guard against creating materialistic attitudes in our own children's lives.

Second, those of us who do not have as much as others, and who will never have as much, must be on guard against the temptation to be envious and judgmental of those who have more than we do. This kind of response can be just as harmful to a person's spiritual growth as a materialistic attitude. In fact, it *is* a materialistic attitude. As Howard Hendricks once said, "Materialism has nothing to do with amount, but it has everything to do with attitude."

Third, we must guard against becoming materialistic by being good stewards of what God *has* given us. What we give to God's work out of what we have is a true test of where we are in our knowledge of God's will and our obedience to His will.

Many Christians do not give as God desires because they don't know what God expects. The Scriptures are clear that He wants all Christians to give regularly and proportionately to His.work from their material resources. This is commanded in the Old Testament as well as in the New.

How much should a Christian give? I personally believe that God established a principle early in the history of the human race—the principle of the tithe, which literally means 10 percent. God commanded the children of Israel to give 10 percent of their material resources to be specifically used to maintain a spiritual ministry among them. It is true that they were to give other tithes as well, this had to do with other aspects of their existence. In many respects, the other tithes could be equated with taxation in our culture. The facts are that 10 percent was given to the Levites in order to carry on a spiritual ministry. When the children of Israel gave 10 percent, God honored them and God's work flourished. When they did not, God did not honor them and God's work floundered. We've already noted this from the passage in Malachi.

The New Testament speaks of regular and proportional giving as God has prospered us. It is only logical that what worked in Israel to carry out the work of God would also be true in a church. And pragmatically that is true. When Christians give 10 percent of their income to the church, the church never lacks for money to meet spiritual needs. When Christians do not give 10 percent, they set limitations on what God wants to do in the local church.

But more important, when a Christian is not obedient in this area of life he is setting limitations on what God wants to do in his own life. And I believe he is setting limitations on what God wants to do through the Body of Christ.

God will bless people who are obedient. He blesses spiritually and He blesses materially. I personally believe that if we are down to our last cup of soup, God will bless us if we share one-tenth of that soup with someone else who is in need. The Scriptures tell us that not even a cup of cold water goes unnoticed by God (Matt. 10:42).

If you do not give *at least* 10 percent of your income to the Lord's work (many Christians give more), I would like to challenge you to do so—to step out by faith. Don't wait until the end of the month to see what's left. Chances are there will be very little, if any. Give it first—before you spend anything for your own needs.

Further, don't wait for a desire to give 10 percent. It probably will never come, especially if you've not been giving this much regularly. This is also true in other areas of obedience. We must learn the *joy of serving* God by *serving.* We must learn the *joy of giving* by *giving.*

I know this was true in my own life. I had not been taught to tithe. My wife had been taught this biblical pattern since she was a very little girl. And after we married, since she was very apt at handling finances, I turned that responsibility over to her. She automatically took 10 percent out of our income and gave it to God's work. Actually, I had not counted on that happening. Initially I didn't *feel* very good about it, especially since I could enumerate many, many things we needed just to get started in life—a car, furniture, new clothes, etc. But I submitted to her desires—somewhat reluctantly. Though there were many things we really wanted and in some instances even needed, we never missed our tithe—and never have since we began. And very soon I learned the joy of giving, even though we had to wait for some of the things *we wanted,* and in some instances some of the things *we needed,* but which were not necessary for survival.

Mary Crowley's testimony is unique in this sense. Mary has built a small door-to-door home accessory line into Home Interiors and Gifts, Incorporated, a national concern based in Dallas with annual sales of over $100,000,000! But what is unique is Mary's struggle when, as a single parent, she did not have enough money to take care of her own needs. She tells about her own struggle at that time.

> There was just no way that I could tithe. Sitting at the kitchen table after the children were asleep, I figured up the stack of bills, my budget

for groceries, rent and housekeeper expenses, the bus fare for going to work and to church on Sundays and Wednesdays. If I added 10 percent of my salary to the debit side of my budget, there would be nothing at all left in the miscellaneous column—no money for Christmas presents, books for the kids, or the dentist. Oh, why did children have to have cavities?

"Lord, You see how it is," I prayed. "I want to tithe, but I don't have enough to take care of the kids as it is."

The answer, as answers to prayer often are, was not what I expected.

"Well, Mary," it seemed God was saying to me, "it looks as though you're not doing such a hot job of providing for the kids by yourself. Why don't you give Me a chance?"

Why not? But I was no dummy in mathematics. I had made good grades in my night accounting class. I knew exactly how much money was in my paycheck from the insurance company where I processed premiums and claims all day. I had memorized fixed expenses. There were always unexpected things such as dentist bills coming along, too.

"Lord, You know I haven't enough," I argued.

"Don't you trust Me, Mary?" God asked.

"Well, yes, but . . . " I was literally pacing the floor that night wrestling with an angel. By the time I signed my name on the pledge card for exactly 10 percent of my salary, the clock had already struck midnight and I was exhausted.

But somehow it was a great relief. I didn't

know how God was going to do more with nine-tenths of my salary than I could do with ten-tenths, but somehow I felt He was going to do it.[1]

Mary goes on to tell how God did just that! And of course the story of her life is well known. She combined faith with good hard work. Today Mary Crowley is able to give far beyond one-tenth of her income to the Lord's work—and she does! She's probably one of the most benevolent Christian women in the world today.

The joy in her life as it relates to her Christian faith began with a decision as to how she was going to give. She struggled with that decision, but she made it. And God blessed her, and He will bless any Christian who is obedient.

WHAT ABOUT YOU?
(James 1:9)

Will you make this decision today? You don't need a pledge card from your church to make that decision. All you need to do is to decide that you will.

Note

1. Mary C. Crowley, *Think Mink* (Old Tappan, NJ: Fleming H. Revell Company, 1976), pp. 33-34.

5
Who Will Receive the "Crown of Life"?

Blessed is the man who perseveres under trial, because when he has stood the test, he will receive the crown of life that God has promised to those who love him (James 1:12).

Before looking in depth at James 1:12, note the definite correlation between this verse and what James taught in verses 2 and 3. He made this continuity clear with at least four words—*joy, trials, perseverance,* and *testing.*

James 1:2-3	*James 1:12*
Consider it pure *joy,* my brothers, when you face *trials* of many kinds, because you know the *testing* of your faith develops *perseverance.*	*Blessed* [joyful] is the man who *perseveres* under *trial,* because when he has stood the *test,* he will receive the crown of life that God has prepared for those who love Him.

There is another point of continuity, but it is more subtle. The Christian who perseveres in difficult circumstances will become "mature and complete." Here James is referring primarily to spiritual growth as we live our lives from day to day. But eventually that maturity will be ultimate. We'll be absolutely and totally complete because we'll be with Jesus Christ in heaven. To quote James, we will receive the "crown of life."

Paul stated it another way, personalizing this truth in his own life. Writing from a Roman prison and knowing he was soon to depart this life, he said: "I have fought the good fight, I have finished the race, I have kept the faith. Now there is in store for me the *crown of righteousness*, which the Lord, the righteous Judge, will award to me on that day" (2 Tim. 4:7-8).

There is no question but that James—and Paul—were speaking of our eternal reward in heaven. Rather than spending eternity separated *from* God, we'll spend eternity *with* God. And as Esther Rusthoi once wrote:

It will be worth it all when we see Jesus,
Life's trials will seem so small when we see Christ;
One glimpse of His dear face all sorrow will erase,
So bravely run the race till we see Christ.[1]

This leads to a very important question. Who will receive the "crown of life"? Being more specific, how can a person be sure he'll spend eternity with Christ?

Over the years this has been a much discussed question. There are many people who, if asked whether or not they were going to spend eternity in heaven, would say, "I hope so." Or they might say, "If my good works outweigh my bad works, I think I'll make it." Or they might respond, "No one can really be sure, but if we *persevere* we'll probably make it." And they may just quote James 1:12 to prove their point.

Is this what James is saying? If so it would not offer much hope to Christians who are already suffering deeply because of persecution. *Trying* to live for Christ in order to *earn salvation* is really a very miserable and discouraging existence.

I was reared in a religious background where I was taught that very thing. And even though I initially put my faith in Christ for salvation, for several years of my life I believed I kept myself saved by what I did. Consequently, my Christian life was like a roller coaster. If I felt I did enough good works to please God, I felt secure. If I felt I was failing to do everything God wanted me to do, and to be everything God wanted me to be, I felt insecure. I thought I may have lost my personal relationship with Jesus Christ.

Another important factor in this up-and-down existence involved my feelings. If I felt happy and joyful and emotionally high, I was quite sure I was a Christian. If I felt unhappy, sad, and depressed, I was very concerned that I may not be a Christian. I was in bondage to my feelings. Since I was going through my adolescent years, which are *normally* characterized by a lot of highs and lows emotionally, I was frequently a miserable young man. Furthermore, since I was quite *idealistic* in terms of what a Christian should be like, I was in double trouble. Even my criteria for measuring spirituality was inaccurate.

What then is James teaching? He's saying several things.

A TRUE TEST
A person who claims to be a Christian and who does

not give up his faith in the midst of trials and difficulties is a *true* Christian. His very *perseverance* proves the reality of his relationship with Jesus Christ.

Pliny, Roman governor in Asia Minor in the early second century, was so puzzled about the Christians who were brought before him for trial that he wrote his famous letter to the emperor Trajan asking for his advice. This was the kind of thing he found himself up against:

A certain unknown Christian was brought before him, and Pliny, finding little fault in him, proceeded to threaten him. "I will banish thee," he said.

"Thou canst not," was the reply. "For all the world is my Father's house."

"Then I will slay thee," said the governor.

"Thou canst not," answered the Christian, "for my life is hid with Christ in God."

"I will take away thy possessions," continued Pliny.

"Thou canst not, for my treasure is in heaven."

"I will drive thee away from man and thou shall have no friend left," was the final threat.

And the calm reply once more was, "Thou canst not, for I have an unseen Friend, from whom thou art not able to separate me."

What was a poor, harassed Roman governor, with all the powers of life and death, torture and the stake at his disposal, to do with people like that?

The facts are that over the centuries many followers of Christ have faced this kind of threat and persecution. And many have stood firm while being martyred, never denying their faith in Jesus Christ. Their perseverance proved the reality of their faith. And even if they had wavered and succumbed to human weakness, God would not have failed them even if they had failed Him. It is one thing to stumble and fall in the Christian life. It is yet another thing to deny the existence of God and His Son, Jesus Christ. A true

Christian can *never* in his heart deny the Lord Jesus Christ
in this sense. And thus we demonstrate that we are truly
His children.

MOTIVATION TO PERSEVERE

The fact that we *have* the promise of eternal life is the
very thing that gives the Christian the motivation to persevere in the midst of trial.

This was Paul's hope. Thus when he too stood before a
Roman emperor, not knowing the outcome, he wrote to
the Philippians, "I eagerly expect and hope that I will in no
way be ashamed, but will have sufficient courage so that
now as always Christ will be exalted in my body, whether
by life or by death. For to me, to live is Christ and to die is
gain" (Phil. 1:20-21).

The apostle Peter spoke to this issue as well when
writing to another group of Christians who were being
persecuted for their faith in Christ. "Praise be to the God
and Father of our Lord Jesus Christ!" he exclaimed. "In
his great mercy he *has given* us new birth into a living hope
through the resurrection of Jesus Christ from the dead,
and into an inheritance that *can never perish, spoil* or
fade—kept in heaven for you, who through faith are
shielded by God's power until the coming of *the salvation*
that is ready to be revealed in the last time" (1 Pet. 1:3-5).

Note that this salvation *was already given* to the people. It was an inheritance that would *never* perish. It was
being *kept* in heaven, not by Christ's followers on earth,
but by God Himself. Consequently, Peter stated that it
was possible for these Christians to "greatly rejoice" even
though they were suffering "all kinds of trials."

And what was the purpose of these trials? Peter
answers that question directly. "These have come so that
your faith—of greater worth than gold, which perishes
even though refined by fire—may be *proved genuine* and

may result in praise, glory and honor when Jesus Christ is revealed" (1 Pet. 1:7).

This statement by Peter relates to the lesson we've already considered. Perseverance in the midst of suffering is indeed a true test of a person's relationship with Jesus Christ. His faith has proved to be "genuine."

Peter underscores the surety of their salvation even more so in his final statements in this paragraph. "Though you have not seen him, you love him;" he wrote, "and even though you do not see him now, you believe in him and are filled with an inexpressible and glorious joy, for you are receiving the goal of your faith, the salvation of your souls" (1 Pet. 1:8-9).

It is estimated that more than fifty million Christians died for their faith in the Dark Ages. It is estimated that a million Christians died for their faith when the Communists seized China. Unnumbered thousands died as martyrs in the revolutions and civil wars in Africa. Why? Because they had hope beyond this life. This was the basis of their motivation and courage. With Paul they were saying, "For to me, to live is Christ and to die is gain" (Phil. 1:21).

A SIGN OF LOVE

Those who "persevere under trial" are those who truly love God.

Peter emphasized the same truth in the passage we've just considered. "Though you have not seen him," Peter wrote, "you *love him*" (1 Pet. 1:8).

There are many people who claim to be Christians, but when their relationship with God is measured by the biblical criterion of *love* they come up wanting.

What does it mean to "love God" in this sense? Jesus answered this question one day for a young, astute Pharisee. The Pharisee asked the Lord what was the greatest commandment in the law. Jesus responded with two basic statements: " 'Love the Lord your God with all your heart and with all your soul and with all your mind.' This is the *first* and greatest commandment. And the *second* is like it: 'Love your neighbor as yourself.' "

Jesus then concluded with another statement that in some respects is mind-boggling, "All the Law and the Prophets," He said, "hang on these two commandments" (Matt. 22:35-40).

With this conclusion, Jesus was defining what it means to love God. If we have a valid relationship with Him through Jesus Christ we will obey His commandments, and this is a reflection of our love (John 15:9-10). A person who loves God and his fellowmen in this way will also obey all the other commandments. We will not worship other gods. We will not take God's name in vain. We will not commit murder or live adulterous lives. We will not steal from others, or lie, or covet what others have. We will honor others—especially our parents (Exod. 20:1-17).

Does this mean we will receive the "crown of life" *because* we have obeyed God's laws? Not at all. Rather, we obey His commandments because we *have* eternal life— and because we love Him. We recognize that God's requirements were fulfilled by Jesus Christ. He paid the death penalty for us because, as Paul stated, no one can keep the law perfectly (Rom. 3:19-20). And if we cannot keep the law perfectly, we cannot inherit eternal life in this way. Only Jesus Christ, God's Son, could do that. And He did, paying the penalty for our sin on the cross.

Some day all Christians, then, will receive the "crown of life" because they have responded to God's love by putting their faith in Christ and then continuing to love God by obeying His commandments. The "crown of life" will be given to all believers some day, not because of our perseverance per se, but because we are true believers, reflecting that reality *with* our perseverance. Even in the midst of severe trials, we remain true to Him.

THE TWENTIETH-CENTURY CHRISTIAN

Once again, those of us who have always lived in the free world face the problem of being able to identify with the trials of the New Testament Christians and those who lived during the centuries immediately following this period. There are, however, several lessons that we *can* identify with.

First, even though our trials may be of a different kind than those of the early Christians who faced severe persecution, we too need to be *sure* of our eternal salvation. If we are not, even the ordinary pressures and problems of life will cause us a lot of emotional and spiritual insecurity. God does not want us to live a hope-so kind of existence. He wants us to *know* that we have eternal life.

Queen Victoria had attended a service in Saint Paul's Cathedral and heard a sermon that had interested her greatly; then she asked her chaplain, "Can one in this life be absolutely sure of eternal safety?" His answer was that he "knew of no way that one could be absolutely sure."

This was published in the court news and fell under the eye of a humble minister of the gospel, John Townsend. He was an intimate friend of George Müeller, whose life of faith led to the founding of his well-known orphanages.

After reading Queen Victoria's question and the answer she received, John Townsend thought and prayed much about the matter, then sent the following note to the queen:

> To her gracious Majesty, our beloved Queen Victoria, from one of her most humble subjects:
> With trembling hands, but heartfilled love, and because I know that we can be absolutely

sure even now of our eternal life in the Home that Jesus went to prepare, may I ask your Most Gracious Majesty to read the following passages of Scripture: John 3:16, Romans 10:9,10?

These passages prove there is full assurance of salvation by faith in our Lord Jesus Christ for those who believe and accept His finished work.

There are many other Scriptures, of course, that could be included. Let me share one of my favorites, which are the words of the apostle Paul to the Romans: "For I am convinced that neither death nor life, neither angels nor demons, neither the present nor the future, nor any powers, neither height nor depth, nor anything else in all creation, will be able to separate us from the love of God that is in Christ Jesus our Lord" (Rom. 8:38-39).

Second, every Christian living in the free world should evaluate his commitment to Christ in the light of New Testament experience. The following questions will help:

1. Does my life really reflect the life of Jesus Christ?
2. Does my commitment to Christ prove the reality of my relationship with Christ?
3. How do I respond to the problems I do face?
   - How bold am I to let people know that I'm a Christian, especially when their life-style contradicts what I believe and what the Bible teaches?
   - How willing am I to take a stand for what is right, even though it may mean rejection?
4. How much do I really love God?
   - Do I love Him with all my heart, my soul, and my mind?
   - How is this love reflected in my life?

5. How much do I think about eternity and the coming of Christ? Or am I so involved in the world system that I think very little about my ultimate hope?

Note
1. *Great Hymns of the Faith* (Grand Rapids: Singspiration, Zondervan Publishing House, 1968), p. 149.

6
Who Is Responsible for Temptation?

When tempted, no one should say, "God is tempt-
ing me." For God cannot be tempted by evil, nor
does he tempt anyone; but each one is tempted
when, by his own evil desire, he is dragged away
and enticed. Then, after desire has conceived, it
gives birth to sin; and sin, when it is full-grown,
gives birth to death (James 1:13-15).

There is within all of us a tendency to blame others for
our problems and mistakes. This should not surprise us,
since our forefather Adam engaged in this kind of behavior
after he yielded to temptation, and with his wife, Eve,
introduced sin into the world. God had clearly instructed

them not to eat fruit from the "tree of the knowledge of good and evil" which He had planted in the garden. Satan first tempted Eve and she succumbed. She then tempted Adam and he succumbed.

God then spoke to Adam, confronting him with his sin. Adam's response is classic and has been a pattern both men and women have followed ever since. Rather than admitting his own mistake he blamed Eve. It was "the *woman you* put here with me," Adam responded. "*She* gave me some fruit from the tree, and I ate it" (Gen. 3:12). And ever since that day, one of the most difficult things for a man or woman to do is to say, "*I'm* guilty! *I'm* wrong! It's *my* fault!"

Have you ever noticed how this happens on the highway? Driving automobiles seems to bring out more of what we are really like than anything else we do. For example, I've seen drivers pull out in front of someone without looking. Tires squeal, horns blow, and oncoming cars brake to a screeching halt. Then comes the classic response! The one who caused it all turns and looks, conveying either verbally or visually (or both), "What's your problem? Who do you think you are trying to run me down?" Some people actually have the uncanny ability of making other people feel guilty for their mistakes.

BLAMING GOD
(James 1:13)

How quickly we tend to blame others. It's a built-in response, with us ever since Adam rationalized his own sin. Adam not only blamed Eve, but ultimately he blamed God. It was "the woman *you* put here with me," he said. And unfortunately, men and women down through the ages have done the same thing. We tend to blame God as well. Thus James said, "When tempted, no one should say, 'God is tempting me' " (Jas. 1:13).

"God Cannot Be Tempted by Evil"

God is "untemptable." He has never experienced evil, nor can He! He is absolutely holy and righteous. The prophet Isaiah refers to Jehovah as the "Holy One" some thirty times. In fact, God's holiness is the primary message of the Old Testament. Consider the following statements:

- "For this is what the high and lofty One says—he who lives forever, whose name is *holy*: 'I live in a high and *holy* place' " (Isa. 57:15).
- "Exalt the Lord our God and worship at his *holy* mountain, for the Lord our God is *holy*" (Ps. 99:9).
- "Your eyes are too *pure* to look on evil; you cannot tolerate wrong" (Hab. 1:13).

"Nor Does He [God] Tempt Anyone"

God not only cannot be "tempted by evil," but neither "does he tempt" any of His creatures. That is, God does not solicit men and women to do evil. Spiros Zodhiates said it well: "God will never deliberately lead you to commit sin, for that would be completely contrary to His original and ever-present desire and yearning to have His creature be fully in the image of the Creator."[1]

Who then is responsible for wrong responses? James answers that question in his next statement.

THE ORIGIN OF WRONG ATTITUDES AND ACTIONS
(James 1:14)

Sinful behavior originates in the heart of every individual. "Each one is tempted," wrote James, "when, by his own evil desire, he is dragged away and enticed" (Jas. 1:14).

As we've just seen, we cannot blame God for our attitudes and actions. Neither can we blame other people!

Nor can we blame our circumstances! We can't even blame Satan! *We* are responsible!

It is true that Satan is a tempter. This is clearly illustrated in the life of Jesus Christ when, for forty days, "He was *tempted* by the devil" (Luke 4:2). Three times Satan attempted to get Jesus to respond to his evil suggestions. But three times Jesus resisted him (Luke 4:3-12). Consequently, we read, "When the devil had finished *all this tempting,* he left him until an opportune time (Luke 4:13).

Though Satan *does* tempt men and women to sin, we are responsible for our responses. And, of course, the temptation may not come directly from Satan as it did in Christ's experience, but from other factors in our environment. The world is permeated with people, activities, objects, and a multitude of auditory and visual stimuli that tempt people to sin. Behind it all is Satan's evil influence. His worldly schemes are present everywhere. And as Paul wrote to the Ephesians, "Our struggle is not against flesh and blood, but against the rulers, against the authorities, against the powers of this dark world and against the spiritual forces of evil in the heavenly realms" (Eph. 6:12).

What causes a person to respond to Satan's schemes in inappropriate ways? James answers this question as well. "Each one is tempted when, by *his own evil desire,* he is dragged away and enticed (Jas. 1:14).

There is within each one of us a capacity to respond in evil ways. The Scriptures call this capacity our "old nature." Paul identified it as the "old man" or the "old self." Writing to the Ephesian Christians he said, "You were taught, with regard to your former way of life, to put off your *old self,* which," he said, "is being corrupted by its *deceitful* desires; to be made new in the attitude of your minds; and to put on the *new self,* created to be like God in true righteousness and holiness" (Eph. 4:22-24). The source of our "evil desires" then is the old nature which resides in every individual born since Adam.

For the Ephesians, this capacity had taken on specific content—sinful attitudes and actions. And this, of course, happens automatically as a person grows and matures chronologically. What we take into our growing minds and hearts forms our behavior. Inherent in this capacity and growth is "desire," which quickly can become evil. Ever since Adam and Eve sinned, our natural tendency is to respond to evil rather than to good. If this is not counterbalanced with God's truth taught directly and modeled in an exemplary fashion, the end result will eventually be a full-blown life-style reflecting "*the desires* of the sinful nature" (Gal. 5:16).

James, then, lays the responsibility for inappropriate responses to temptations squarely on our shoulders. If we nourish "evil desire" in our lives, it will soon take over and we will begin responding in sinful ways. And this leads us to James's conclusion in verse 15.

THE RESULTS OF YIELDING TO TEMPTATION (James 1:15)

Let's summarize! God does not tempt people to sin. Rather, every individual is tempted when he yields to his own evil desire. "Then," James concludes, "after desire has conceived, it gives birth to sin; and sin, when it is full-grown, gives birth to death" (Jas. 1:15).

Temptation and "evil desire" per se are not sin. Sin results when we are "dragged away and enticed." And at this point, sin is born.

Here James uses an interesting analogy. "Evil desire," once it is activated and nourished, "conceives" and "gives birth." What is "born" is sin. And if sin is not dealt with, it will grow and mature and eventually give "birth to death."

In South America there is a strange vine known as the matador. Beginning at the foot of the tree, it slowly makes its way to the top. As it grows, it kills the tree, and when at last the top is reached, it sends forth a flower to crown itself.

Matador means "killer." And the matador plant illustrates graphically the process James described. Take jealousy as an example. It appears harmless when it is small, but if it is allowed to grow, its tendrils of malice and hatred clasp themselves around the heart and eventually "kill" the soul. Thus James wrote, "After desire is conceived, it gives birth to sin; and sin, when it is full-grown, gives birth to death" (Jas. 1:15).

At this point we once again need elaboration, and once again the apostle Paul helps us to understand James's succinct generalization. In his letter to the Galatian Christians, Paul outlined clearly the acts of sin which are born once evil desire conceives. He wrote, "The acts of the sinful nature are obvious: sexual immorality, impurity and debauchery; idolatry and witchcraft; hatred, discord, jealousy, fits of rage, selfish ambition, dissensions, factions and envy; drunkenness, orgies, and the like." And then Paul issues a warning, "Those who live like this will not inherit the kingdom of God" (Gal. 5:19-21).

What is the solution to this problem that lies dormant in the life of every child born into this world, and which will soon become activated as his natural abilities to learn develop and mature? The answer lies in conversion to Jesus Christ. When we become a Christian we receive a new capacity which enables us to serve God and others rather than self. And, once we become born-again believers, if we follow the leadership of the Holy Spirit in our lives, we will more and more reflect the "fruit of the Spirit" (Gal. 5:22) rather than the "acts of the sinful nature" (5:19).

After Paul outlined the "acts of the sinful nature" he also outlined the "fruit of the Spirit." This fruit is "love, joy, peace, patience, kindness, goodness, faithfulness, gentleness and self-control" (Gal. 5:22-23).

THE TWO NATURES

What happens to the old capacity when a Christian receives this new capacity?

Once, the great French preacher Bourdaloue was probing the conscience of Louis XIV, applying to him the words of Paul in Romans 7:19 and intending to paraphrase them: "For the good which I would, I do not, but the evil which I would not, that I do." He began: "I find two men in me . . ."

The king then interrupted the great preacher with the memorable exclamation: "Ah, these two men, I know them well!"

All of us as Christians can echo this same experience. We too know them well! When we become Christians, the old nature is still present in our lives. However, we do not have to serve this old nature. "Those who belong to Christ Jesus have crucified the sinful nature with its passions and desires," wrote Paul (Gal. 5:24). The old nature need not rise up and control us. We will still be tempted—just as Jesus was tempted—and we still have evil desires, but we do not need to succumb to that temptation and be led astray. As someone has said, "We cannot keep the birds from flying over our heads, but we can keep the birds from making nests in our hair." Just so, we cannot eliminate all sinful influences in our lives, but we can keep from yielding to those influences and allowing them to set up residency in our lives.

PRACTICAL SUGGESTIONS FOR DEALING WITH TEMPTATIONS

First, we must not blame God for our temptations, evil desires and sinful actions. To do so leads to rationalization.

For example, there are those who say, "Since God made me this way, I have no choice."

This leads to a question that's been debated for centuries. Since God created all things, isn't He responsible for evil and sin? The answer is definitely no. We can never satisfactorily explain why He is *not* the author of evil any more than we can satisfactorily explain the fact that Jesus Christ was both God and man. We only know that "God cannot be tempted by evil, nor does he tempt anyone." Adam and Eve were responsible for their actions. And so are we!

Second, we must realize and accept the fact that as Christians, we have two natures. This is a reality. We will always have conflict in our lives. Furthermore, the intensity of this conflict is often related to our life-style before we became Christians. Unfortunately, Paul was right, "A man reaps what he sows" (Gal. 6:7).

Perhaps more difficult to accept is the fact that we also reap what others sow in our lives—misguided parents, the wrong kind of friends, and many evil people in this world. But we are still responsible for our sinful actions. No matter how intense the conflict between our old and new natures, we must follow the leadership of the Holy Spirit rather than the desires of the old nature.

Third, we must avoid situations and circumstances that stir up evil desires. All of us are vulnerable in different areas in our lives. We know what these areas are. And if we continually subject ourselves to stimuli that trigger evil desires, we are simply asking for trouble. The psalmist said, "Blessed is the man who does not *walk* in the counsel of the wicked or *stand* in the way of sinners or *sit* in the seat of mockers" (Ps. 1:1).

And note! If we walk in the midst of people and things that cause temptation, it's easy to stop—and stand—and watch—and feed the evil desires that are activated by what we see. And before we know it, we are *sitting* in the midst of those who are sinning—*and* participating. We must turn our back on temptation and run the other way. This is what Joseph did when he was sorely tempted by Potiphar's wife. He eventually would not even be in her presence. And when she tried to seduce him on one occasion, he turned and ran out of the house (Gen. 39:10-12). But unfortunately, however, E.C. McKenzie was right when he said, "Few speed records are broken when people run from temptation."

Fourth, we must use God's Word to resist temptation. The psalmist, after saying that a man is blessed if he "does not walk in the counsel of the wicked or stand in the way of sinners or sit in the seat of mockers" gives a beautiful and profound contrast. The man or woman who resists temptation finds that their "delight is in the law of the Lord." This person "meditates day and night" upon God's Word. The result is that this person "is like a tree planted by streams of water, which yields its fruit in season and whose leaf does not wither. Whatever he does prospers" (Ps. 1:2-3).

Remember how Jesus Christ responded to Satan when He was tempted in the wilderness? Three times the Lord responded with Scripture to Satan's specific requests. "It is written . . . It is written . . . It is written . . . ," He said. And eventually Satan turned and left Him alone.

Satan cannot ultimately resist God's Word. He succumbs. As Christians we need to learn Scripture and make it a part of our minds and hearts. Thus when we face temptation we must meditate on that Scripture and use it to redirect our thoughts and desires—and actions.

Fifth, we must realize that Jesus Christ can identify with every temptation we face. Again, we cannot understand or explain this reality. We've seen that God is "untemptable," but when He became a man in the person of Jesus Christ, He *was* tempted. The author of the book of Hebrews tells us that Jesus Christ, in His human nature, was "tempted in every way, just as we are." Yet, He "was without sin." He *never* yielded to temptation (Heb. 4:15). This may sound contradictory, but it is no more so than the fact that "God is Spirit" (John 4:24), and yet He "became flesh and lived for a while among us" (John 1:14). This is one of those many unfathomable mysteries in Christian theology.

The facts are that Jesus Christ can identify with every temptation every person in every situation throughout history has faced. This is why He now sits at the right hand of God as a High Priest who can "sympathize with our weaknesses" (Heb. 4:15) so that "we may receive mercy and find grace to help us in our time of need" (Heb. 4:16). And let us also remember the encouraging words of Paul who wrote that "no temptation has seized you except what is common to man. And God is faithful; he will not let you be tempted beyond what you can bear. But when you are tempted, he will also provide a way out so that you can stand up under it (1 Cor. 10:13).

Sixth, we must be on guard at all times against Satan's evil schemes. We are often most vulnerable when we have been most successful in living the Christian life. It's at that point we're tempted to let our guard down.

Stewart Anderson, when preaching on temptation, reminds us that Bobby Leach, the Englishman, startled the world by going over Niagara Falls in a barrel without suffering serious harm. Some years later he was walking down the street, slipped on an orange peel, and was taken to the hospital with a badly fractured leg. Dr. Anderson adds: "Some great temptations, which roar around us like Niagara may leave us unharmed. But a little, insignificant incident may cause our downfall simply because we're not looking for it."

A PERSONAL COMMITMENT

With God's help, I will not blame Him for my temptations, evil desires, and sinful actions. Realizing I have two natures, I will follow the leadership of the Holy Spirit in my life rather than my sinful desires. I will avoid situations and circumstances that stir up evil desires. I will learn more of God's Word and commit it to memory in order to resist temptation. Realizing that Jesus Christ can identify with every temptation I face, I will constantly look to Him in prayer, asking Him to help me resist temptation. Furthermore, I will be on guard at all times against Satan's evil schemes, realizing that I can be victorious over evil if I will "be strong in the Lord and in his mighty power" and "put on the full armor of God" as outlined in His Word (Eph. 6:10-18).

Note

1. Spiros Zodhiates, *The Behavior of Belief* (Grand Rapids: Wm. B. Eerdmans Publishing Company, 1959), p. 65.

7
How Can We Keep from Being Deceived?

Don't be deceived, my dear brothers. Every good and perfect gift is from above, coming down from the Father of the heavenly lights, who does not change like shifting shadows. He chose to give us birth through the word of truth, that we might be a kind of firstfruits of all he created (James 1:16-18).

In what ways can a person—even a Christian—be deceived? A look at the scriptural context of each warning against deception helps us to answer this question rather specifically, beginning with James's statement itself.

"DON'T BE DECEIVED" (James 1:16)

Know the Source of Evil Desire
James's main concern in the context of his warning against deception is that a Christian understand the source

of sin—it originates deep within our own hearts. He warns against blaming God for our evil desires and, more so, our sinful actions. To misunderstand this reality will surely lead to self-deception and persistent rationalization. Furthermore, it will open the door to all kinds of departure from the will of God.

False Religious Leaders

Jesus warned against "false Christs" (Matthew 24:24). There will be those who will actually claim to be the Messiah. "Many will come in my name," Jesus said, "claiming, 'I am the Christ,' and will *deceive* many" (24:5).

Jesus' warning was actually an answer to a question asked by His disciples relative to the second coming of Christ. It is clearly implied in this passage that the number of false teachers and leaders will increase as we move towards "the end of the age" (Matt. 24:3).

Someone has reported that there have been more than a thousand leaders in different parts of the world in the last fifty years who have claimed to be Christ and the Saviour of the world. Most of these false Christs have risen in Africa, India, or the Orient and have spread into the West. However, there are also many false religions that have grown out of historic Christianity itself. America alone has more than 350 sects and cults, and most of them claim to base their doctrines on the teachings of the Bible.

Occultism has also increased rapidly in recent years. In many respects this movement has spread concurrently with a growing belief in astrology. Someone has reported that one American in five expresses belief in astrology. Occult book sales have flourished. At one point in time, more than 800 different titles were available. One of the busiest bookstores is the Metaphysical Center in San Francisco, which offers courses in palmistry, reincarnation, astral projection, numerology, and others. Another bookstore sells ritual robes, amulets, incense, crystal balls, etc.

All of this points to one conclusion. Millions of people have been and are being deceived and led astray regarding who Jesus Christ really is. Thus John wrote, "Dear children, this is the last hour; and as you have heard that the antichrist is coming, even now many antichrists have come . . . . Who is the liar? It is the man who denies that Jesus is the Christ. Such a man is the antichrist—he denies the Father and the Son. No one who denies the Son has the Father; whoever acknowledges the Son has the Father also" (1 John 2:18,22-23).

It is interesting to note that most religious cults today, including the large movements identified as Mormonism and Jehovah's Witnesses, deny the doctrine of the Trinity—that God the Father, God the Son, and God the Holy Spirit are one God and yet three Persons. They do not believe that Jesus Christ was one with God nor do they believe that He *was* God.

Furthermore, many mainline Protestant ministers also deny many of the great doctrines of Christianity. Several years ago, *McCalls* magazine reported on a survey of 3,000 Protestant clergymen. The *McCalls* article stated: "A considerable number rejected altogether the idea of a personal God. God, they said, was the Ground of Being, the Force of Life, the Principle of Love, Ultimate Reality and so forth. A majority of the youngest group of ministers cannot be said to believe in the virgin birth or to regard Jesus as divine."

Don't Live According to the Sinful Nature

There's another great area of deception described in Scripture which relates more specifically to James's overriding concern. It often grows out of a wrong view of who Jesus Christ really is, but not necessarily. In fact, there are those whose basic doctrines regarding the Godhead and salvation are above reproach, but yet they are deceived in how they actually live the Christian life. Thus the Bible speaks very directly to this issue.

The Corinthians are a prime example. When they first heard the gospel, their life-style was characterized by all sorts of wickedness and evil. Many responded to the message of Christ, but a number of them continued to live sinful lives even though they chose to follow Christ. Paul wrote, "Do you not know that the wicked will not inherit the kingdom of God? *Do not be deceived:* Neither the sexually immoral nor idolators nor adulterers nor male prostitutes nor homosexual offenders nor thieves nor the greedy nor drunkards nor slanderers nor swindlers will inherit the kingdom of God. *And that is what some of you were.* But you were washed, you were sanctified, you were justified in the name of the Lord Jesus Christ and by the Spirit of our God" (1 Cor. 6:9-11).

The problem, of course, is that they had not yet "put off" their "old self" and "put on" the "new self" (Eph. 4:22-24). They were in a constant state of deception. Those whose relationship with Christ was authentic eventually responded to Paul's teachings and exhortation on godliness and holiness. In his second letter Paul commended the Corinthians for their godly response and spirit of repentance (2 Cor. 7:8-16).

The fact that we are Christians does not mean that we cannot be deceived and led astray in the areas enumerated by Paul. For example, even Christians who have followed Christ faithfully for years have succumbed to sexual temptation. Some admit that they have sinned. Others continue to rationalize their behavior as an acceptable "Christian" practice.

I have in my files some letters from a man who had read the book I wrote entitled *The Measure of a Man.* In one chapter I deal with marital faithfulness, which relates to Paul's statement that a Christian man should be faithful to his wife—truly a "man of one woman." The man I'm referring to wrote two lengthy letters filled with Scripture, attempting to convince me that it is perfectly all right for a married man to have regular sex relationships with other women, so long as they are single women. In that sense he was trying to convince me—and himself—that he was not committing adultery. This is the most classic example of deception relative to what the Bible teaches about sexual morality that I have ever encountered.

Many of us may shake our heads in unbelief at this kind of self-deception. But may I remind you that there is within us all a tendency to cover our sins. Though this man's behavior is extreme, it illustrates the way in which many of us justify our sinful actions. Sexual morality versus immorality may not be the issue. Rather, it may relate to honesty versus dishonesty; a quiet spirit versus anger; wholesome language versus foul language; submission versus dominance and control; materialistic attitudes versus non-materialistic attitudes; and selfishness versus unselfishness. Thus James wrote, "Don't be deceived, my dear brothers." In essence he was saying, "Don't be led astray"; "don't get sidetracked from the truth"; "don't get off the path of righteousness"; "don't violate the will of God."

"EVERY GOOD AND PERFECT GIFT IS FROM ABOVE"
(James 1:17)

Why does James turn his attention to God's gifts after warning Christians to guard against being deceived and led astray? First, he wanted us to know that God can give only gifts that are "good" and "perfect." Because of who He is He cannot be associated with anything that is evil and imperfect. But unfortunately, we can take what is "good" and "perfect" and use it in evil and imperfect ways. But when we do, that does not rob God's gifts of their goodness.

Let me illustrate. What would we do without a knife at home? It's very useful. But if misused it can become deadly. If, for instance, rather than using it to peel potatoes, it is used to take the life of an innocent child, it becomes an evil weapon. In a case like this, of course, we would not arrest the maker of the knife or imprison the knife itself, but we would punish the user of the knife who used it in an evil, sinful way. Thus any of God's good gifts may prove to be evil when we handle those gifts in inappropriate ways.

Take food as an example. It is a wonderful gift from God. But we can use food in sinful ways. We can eat to live or we can live to eat. This does not mean we should not enjoy food. But it does mean we shouldn't overindulge so as to use God's good gifts in purely selfish ways. The Bible consistently warns against gluttony and drunkenness.

Take sex as another example. It is one of God's greatest gifts to mankind. Originally God designed the gift to illustrate His oneness with us—His creatures. But this gift has many other purposes as well—to provide security, to express true love, to give pleasure, and of course, to bring children into the world.

But this good gift can also be used in evil ways. We can prostitute it. We can use it promiscuously, violating God's standards of morality. We can also use it selfishly, even within God's stated boundaries of marriage. We can use it manipulatively in order to control another person. We can use it vindictively to vent our anger.

All of God's gifts are good. The quality never changes. They are righteous and pure and lovely and good. As John states, "God is light; in him there is no darkness at all" (1 John 1:5).

James, in 1:17, uses an illustration from nature to get his point across. These good gifts come "from the Father of the *heavenly lights.*" When the Lord first created the heavens and the earth, "Darkness was over the surface of the deep" (Gen. 1:2). God later created the sun and the moon and the stars and "set them in the expanse of the sky to give light on the earth" (Gen. 1:17).

God's physical creation itself illustrates His nature. He's righteous and holy, and when He came into this world in human form He was identified as the "light of the world" (John 8:12). By contrast, the Scriptures again and again identify sin and evil with "darkness."

James used another illustration from nature—"shifting shadows." The focus here is on human nature. Like shadows that constantly change and shift, we tend to wander from God's straight and narrow path—even as His children. Robert Robinson captured this reality well in his song "Come Thou Fount of Every Blessing."

> Oh to grace how great a debtor
> daily I'm constrained to be!
> Let Thy goodness like a fetter
> bind my wandering heart to Thee.
> Prone to wander—Lord, I feel it—
> prone to leave the God I love;
> Here's my heart—oh take and seal it,
> seal it for Thy courts above.

God, however, "does not change like shifting shadows." He is absolutely constant and immutable in His character. His love is unconditional. His holiness never varies. There is no evil in Him. This is why James stated earlier that "God cannot be tempted by evil, nor does he tempt anyone" (Jas. 1:13).

"HE CHOSE TO GIVE US BIRTH THROUGH THE WORD OF TRUTH"
(James 1:18)

How can we guard against deception and wandering from God's will?

We Must Be Born Again

This is foundational to discovering the perfect will of God. There is a unique passage in Paul's letter to Titus that amplifies on James's statement. "At one time we too were foolish, disobedient, *deceived* and *enslaved* by all kinds of passions and pleasures. We lived in malice and envy, being hated and hating one another. But when the kindness and love of God our Saviour appeared, he saved us, not because of righteous things we had done, but because of his mercy. He saved us through the washing of *rebirth* and renewal by the Holy Spirit" (Titus 3:3-5). When we by faith respond to God's truth and receive Jesus Christ as personal Saviour, He promises to give us eternal life. We are given a *new position*—an eternal position in Christ—as well as a *new capacity* to conform our lives to Jesus Christ even while we continue our sojourn on earth.

We Must Learn the Word of God

God also gives us instructions regarding how to avoid deception as a Christian. The same "word of truth" that the Holy Spirit uses to regenerate our hearts is also able to keep us on God's straight and narrow pathway. Jesus Christ made this point very clear one day while talking to the Sadducees. "You are in error," He said, "because you do not know the Scriptures" (Matt. 22:29).

Paul also made this clear in his second letter to Timothy. First, he stated that "everyone who wants to live a godly life in Christ Jesus will be persecuted." At the same time "evil men and imposters will go from bad to worse, *deceiving* and *being deceived.*"

Paul then exhorts Timothy specifically to "continue in what" he has "learned" and has "become convinced of." He reminded this young man that from a very early age he had "known the *holy Scriptures*"—which first of all made him "wise for *salvation* through faith in Christ Jesus." Furthermore, Paul told Timothy that "all *Scripture* is God-breathed and is useful for teaching, rebuking, correcting and training in righteousness so that the man of God may be thoroughly equipped for every good work" (2 Tim. 3:12-17).

There's only one way to guard against being deceived. We must learn the Word of God consistently. It alone can keep us from being led astray into false doctrine and a lifestyle that is not pleasing to God. The Bible is the only trustworthy source for knowing what to believe and how to live.

We Must Avoid Associations That Lead Us Astray

The Scriptures themselves mention another very important guideline for avoiding deception, particularly in terms of how we live the Christian life. Paul wrote to the Corinthians and said—"Do not be *misled* (deceived): 'bad company corrupts good character' " (1 Cor. 15:33).

All Christians who associate on a regular basis with people who live sinful lives need to be on constant guard against allowing themselves to be like them. This is a problem, of course, because we cannot leave this world, as Paul states in his first letter to the Corinthians (1 Cor. 5:9-11). But we must avoid associating with people where we will be tempted to enter into their activities and function as they do. If we are not careful, we can very quickly find ourselves corrupted in our own hearts. We all need "models of righteousness," not unrighteousness.

IN SUMMARY . . .

James is telling us in this passage to be on guard against deception. We can be led astray both in what we believe and in the way we live. And one way in which Satan tries to deceive us is to cause us to take God's good gifts and use them in evil ways.

To avoid deception, we must first come to Jesus Christ in faith and be born again. Then we must continually conform our lives to the Word of God and avoid associating with people who will corrupt us and lead us astray.

SOME QUESTIONS TO THINK ABOUT

How well do I know what I believe . . .

   . . . about the Bible?

   . . . about God?

   . . . about Jesus Christ (His deity, His incarnation, His substitutionary death, His resurrection, His priestly ministry, His second coming)?

   . . . about the Holy Spirit (His indwelling, His healing, His baptism, His filling)?

   . . . about the Trinity?

   . . . about sin and salvation?

   . . . about Satan?

   . . . about the church?

How well do I discern false doctrine?

How well do I know the will of God for my life as it is outlined in the Bible?

How obedient am I to what I do know?

Am I truly born again?

8
What Is the Basic Secret for a Successful Life?

My dear brothers, take note of this: Everyone should be quick to listen, slow to speak and slow to become angry, for man's anger does not bring about the righteous life that God desires (James 1:19-20).

Once a young man came to the great philosopher Socrates to be instructed in oratory. The moment the young man was introduced he began to talk in an incessant stream. This went on for some time. When Socrates could get in a word he said, "Young man, I will have to charge you a double fee."

"A double fee, why is that?"

The old sage replied, "I will have to teach you two sciences. First, how to hold your tongue, and then, how to use it."

James would have enjoyed this story. More than any other New Testament writer he was concerned about how a Christian uses his tongue. The subject comes up several times in his letter and the passage before us, 1:19-20, is the first occasion.

The primary focus in this brief paragraph is anger, but true to form, James used a few succinct words to dispense a lot of wisdom. There are several secrets to a successful life in these two short verses.

James first established continuity when he wrote, "My dear brothers, take note of this" (1:19). In the previous verse he had reminded his readers that they had been given new life "through the *word of truth*" (1:18). Now he is asking his readers to pay particular attention to the fact that the Word of God is vitally related to what he is about to say. And this gives us a clue as to the *primary meaning* inherent in James's statement "Everyone should be *quick to listen.*"

BE QUICK TO LISTEN

Later we'll see that James has introduced us to a process for controlling anger. But his initial concern was that we be "quick to listen" to *what God has said*. He is not only treating the *process* of listening—which is very important—but also the specific *content* we are to listen to, which is even more important.

Solomon once wrote, "Of making many books there is no end" (Eccles. 12:12). Never before in the history of the world has so much been written and published. There are many voices crying in the wilderness, attempting to get our attention through the printed page as well as through the visual media. And it's true that along with the bad there are many good things being said. But James brings us back to the primary source of all knowledge and wisdom—the Word of God. When God speaks we should be "quick to listen." And He *has spoken* through the Scriptures. If we ignore His voice, we'll suffer the consequences. Unfortunately, most people in the world today are not listening. This is not surprising. But even more unfortunate, many Christians are not listening either.

Listening to God is what Solomon had in mind when again and again, in the book of Proverbs, he warned his readers to pay careful attention to learning. *Listen* to the following statements:

• "A wise man will *hear* and increase in learning, and a man of understanding will *acquire* wise counsel" (Prov. 1:5, *NASB*).
• "*Hear,* my son, your father's instruction, and do not forsake your mother's teaching" (Prov. 1:8, *NASB*).
• "He who *listens* to me shall live securely, and shall be at ease from the dread of evil" (Prov. 1:33, *NASB*).
• "*Make your ear attentive* to wisdom, incline your heart to understanding" (Prov. 2:2, *NASB*).
• "How blessed is the man who finds wisdom, and the man who gains understanding" (Prov. 3:13, *NASB*).

James too is emphasizing how important it is to listen to God's voice through the Word of God. Though there is much wisdom available today, there is no wisdom more basic and important than God's revealed Word.

Paul's words to Timothy emphasize the same message and are just as relevant today as they were the day he wrote them to this young man. "All Scripture is God-breathed and is useful for teaching, rebuking, correcting and training in righteousness, so that the man of God may be thoroughly equipped for every good work" (2 Tim. 3:16-17). And James underscored the same reality when he wrote, "Everyone should be *quick to listen*." God chose to give us birth through the word of truth and if we will continue to listen to His voice and "humbly accept the

word" which is planted within us (Jas. 1:21), we will grow
and mature and face life and its challenges victoriously.

BE SLOW TO SPEAK

James's next statement adds to the formula for a successful life. We are to be "slow to speak." In context this
means that a new Christian should be careful about dispensing knowledge. We may be wise in the ways of the
world, but we may be very unwise when it comes to a
knowledge of God's truth.

This is what James had in mind when he later wrote,
"Not many of you should presume to be teachers, my
brothers, because you know that we who teach will be
judged more strictly" (Jas. 3:1). This, of course, is a
sobering statement for those of us who teach the Word of
God regularly. We will be held accountable for what we say
and how we interpret God's Word.

This warning must be tempered. Many Christians tend
to be intimidated to begin with. Thus James's statement to
be "slow to speak" must not be used to accentuate that
intimidation. In fact, there are many Christians who need
to be encouraged to speak out.

What, then, is James's major concern? This is a warning against prideful behavior. It is easy for Satan to deceive
a new Christian regarding his ability to communicate wisdom to others.

This is what Paul had in mind when he warned Timothy
not to "be hasty in the laying on of hands" (1 Tim. 5:22),
that is, the appointing of spiritual leaders in the church.
Earlier in this same letter he had written that an elder
"must not be a recent convert, or he may become con-
ceited and fall under the same judgment as the devil" (1
Tim. 3:6).

It is dangerous to put new Christians in top-level leadership positions in the church where they are responsible

to lead and guide other people in spiritual matters. It is unfair to them, for we are putting them in a very vulnerable position. In many respects, we're setting them up for a satanic attack. And the area he will attack directly is in the area of pride.

The same thing can happen to younger men, even though they may have been Christians for a long time. However, this does not mean that younger men cannot be effective in God's work. Consider Timothy's classic example. He *was* a young man! But he was also a young man who was "quick to listen" and "slow to speak." He was very much aware of his youthfulness and lack of experience. Thus he looked continually to the apostle Paul, his spiritual father, for wisdom and guidance.

But note again that James is not just singling out *new* Christians and *young* Christians. Rather, he wrote, "*Everyone* should be quick to listen, slow to speak . . . "

I remember hearing Dr. Wilbur Smith, a well-known author and lecturer, talking about Dr. William Culbertson, who served for a number of years as president of Moody Bible Institute. At the time, Dr. Smith was serving on a special Bible translation committee with Dr. Culbertson. "Most of us could learn a great deal from Dr. Culbertson," he stated. "He attends our committee meetings, listens intently to all of the rest of us, and then at some point makes a very wise statement that every one of us wishes we could have made." And, of course, the point Dr. Smith was making is that most of them probably *could* have made the statement had they been listening rather than talking.

Dr. Smith's story impressed me because I had the privilege of sitting in hundreds of faculty meetings at Moody Bible Institute when Dr. Culbertson was president. I recall how often the same thing happened then. We'd spend an hour discussing a very important issue and many of us, particularly those of us who were young, were often "quick to speak" dispersing our pearls of wisdom. Dr. Culbertson would patiently listen for a long period of time, and then finally stand up and, with great sensitivity and real wisdom, succinctly state the solution to the problem.

How often many of us reflected back on what he said and wished we had kept our own mouths shut. And furthermore, had we done so, had we been "quick to listen" and "slow to speak," we'd probably have been able to dispense some of the same wisdom!

BE SLOW TO BECOME ANGRY

James adds a third dimension to this formula for success in life. "Everyone should be quick to listen, slow to speak and *slow to become angry.*" And then James states *why,* "For man's anger does not bring about the righteous life that God desires" (Jas. 1:20).

One of the tendencies we all have when someone disagrees with us is to become impatient and angry. The moment that happens, communication usually breaks down and misunderstandings set in. We've stopped *listening* to one another. Rather than being "slow to speak," we usually are "quick to speak" and frequently what is said is communicated in hurtful and harsh words. Before long, emotion takes over.

On the other hand, dramatic things can happen when one or several people refuse to allow anger to become a dominant force in the communication process. In fact, intense emotions can be dissipated rather quickly. And this should not surprise us in view of what we read in Proverbs 15. "A gentle answer turns away wrath," wrote Solomon, "but a harsh word stirs up anger" (Prov. 15:1).

I'll never forget an experience a number of years ago while participating in a lectureship at a well known theological seminary. While there, I used a school car which had the name of the school imprinted on both sides of the automobile. I was driving out of a parking lot onto a main highway and in the process got confused. It was very difficult to discern where the parking lot ended and the highway began. Before I knew what was happening, I had pulled out and stopped in the middle of the main thoroughfare. At that moment I looked up and saw a car bearing down on me. I knew I was in trouble—in more ways than one. Rather than slowing down, the driver seemed to speed up. I could see the anger in his face through his front windshield—and I'm glad I couldn't read his lips. Just short of broadsiding me he hit the brakes, swerved around me and did a complete 180 as he skidded to a stop. He then jumped out of the car, came storming up to the driver's side of my car, ready to unleash his fury.

I sensed immediately from what he was saying that his anger was intensified because of the name of the seminary imprinted on the side of the car. It was clear his previous encounters with students or faculty or both had not been too pleasant for him. In fact, it seemed to be his opportunity to deal with what he considered hypocrisy—which he proceeded to outline in a rather descriptive, colorful way.

I knew I was in trouble. I also knew I was wrong, though I certainly had not pulled in front of him on purpose. Fortunately, I had presence of mind to immediately apologize for my stupid blunder. "I'm sorry," I said, in a quiet and trembling voice. "I got confused as to where the parking lot ends and the highway begins. I know I'm wrong. All I can do is apologize."

At that moment I saw his anger dissipate. It was a dramatic and instantaneous change. He dropped his head, paused for a moment, and then said softly, "I'm sorry . . . I'm sorry . . . " He then walked to his car, got in and drove away.

I've often reflected back on that event, and every time

I do I think of Proverbs 15:1, "A gentle answer turns away wrath, but a harsh word stirs up anger."

Anger, of course, is a normal emotion. And I can understand this man's reaction. I may have felt the same angry feelings had I been in his position, although I think my behavior would have been somewhat different. (At least I hope so.) And this leads us to a very basic question.

IS ALL ANGER SIN?

All anger is not sinful. Angry feelings per se are *not* sinful. James certainly alludes to this when he exhorts Christians to be "slow to become angry" and then states that "anger does not bring about the righteous life that God desires" (Jas. 1:20). In other words, if we allow anger to become a regular part of our life, it will eventually lead us to behavior that violates God's standards of righteousness—and that certainly is sinful.

The apostle Paul made this point even clearer when he wrote, "*In your anger do not sin,*" and then warned, "Do not let the sun go down while you are still angry, and do not give the devil a foothold" (Eph. 4:26-27).

Aristotle, another great philosopher, once said, "Anyone can become angry. That is easy. But to be angry with the right person, to the right degree, at the right time, and in the right way—that is not easy."

It is possible to be angry without sinning, but if we allow the anger to linger, we are opening the door to Satan who, if he can get his foot in the door, will indeed do all he can to lead us into some kind of unrighteousness and sinful behavior.

We must realize that the capacity to be angry is just as much a part of our God-created nature as the capacity to love. We are made in the image of God, and God Himself has a unique capacity for *both* anger and love. In dealing with anger in our lives, we must realize first of all that it is a normal, God-created emotion.

There are two extreme responses to anger. On the one hand, we tend to repress it in ourselves and in our children. If we do, there is an abundance of evidence that we will create a lot of emotional difficulties. The main manifestation is depression.

The other reaction to anger that is an extreme is to express it and vent it in improper ways. There is also an abundance of evidence that this does not solve the problem. It's true that it's much more effective for small children to vent anger because anger is unsophisticated, spontaneous, and unpremeditated. It usually rises quickly and disappears quickly. A child can be screaming one moment and laughing the next. It holds no grudges.

The same is not true of adults. Our anger is closely intertwined with conscious, deliberate thoughts, and rather complex situations. Simply venting that anger does not resolve the problem. If the causes are not dealt with, venting it only tends to generate more anger. One reason is that we know what we are doing, we enjoy what we are doing, and we are gratifying ourselves in what we are doing to someone else.

WHEN IS ANGER SINFUL?

Anger becomes sinful *when we use it to take revenge.* The Scriptures make it clear that we are not to "repay anyone evil for evil" (Rom. 12:17). When anger causes us to take matters into our own hands in order to get even with someone because of what they've done to us, we are definitely sinning against God. This is retaliation!

When we allow anger to turn to bitterness it becomes sinful. At this point Paul draws a line. After warning the Ephesians to guard against anger lest it become sinful, he said, "Get rid of all bitterness, rage and anger, brawling and slander, along with every form of malice" (Eph. 4:31). At this point, we not only hurt others, we hurt ourselves. Listen to the following Proverbs:

- "He who guards his lips guards his soul, but he who speaks rashly will come to ruin" (Prov. 13:3).
- "A hot-tempered man must pay the penalty; if you rescue him, you will have to do it again" (Prov. 19:19).
- "He who guards his mouth and his tongue keeps himself from calamity" (Prov. 21:23).

When we are quick-tempered we sin. The Bible repeatedly warns against being quick-tempered. Paul was so concerned about this particular quality that he instructed Timothy to avoid appointing men to spiritual leadership who have this weakness (Titus 1:7). The reasons for this concern are also stated clearly in several Proverbs:

- "A quick-tempered man does foolish things" (Prov. 14:17).
- "Like a city whose walls are broken down is a man who lacks self-control" (Prov. 25:28).
- "An angry man stirs up dissensions, and a hot-tempered one commits many sins" (Prov. 29:22).

HOW CAN WE LEARN TO CONTROL ANGER?

The answer to how we can control anger takes us back to the process inherent in James's teaching when he wrote, "Everyone should be quick to listen, slow to speak and slow to become angry." Though he is speaking primarily about being "quick to listen" to the *Word of God*— which as we've seen gives us numerous warnings about the effects of anger—he is also setting before us a *process* that helps to control anger. Many people get angry because they misunderstand what is being said or done by someone else. They don't hear correctly or view the event with understanding. Or if they do hear and see correctly, they don't ask themselves *why* that person is behaving in that way.

There's only one way to gain perspective on another person's angry actions—we must be "quick to listen" and "slow to speak." There are times we must force ourselves *not* to react, to figuratively or literally bite our tongues, and then *listen!*

This process in itself helps to control anger. It is not accidental that James outlined these three steps and in this sequence:

First, be quick to listen.

Second, be slow to speak.

Third, be slow to become angry.

Again, the Proverbs are very helpful in understanding this point. Notice the emphasis in these Scriptures on being "understanding," "having knowledge," as well as "discretion," and how these qualities affect our ability to control anger:

- "He who is slow to anger is better than the mighty, and he who rules his spirit, than he who captures a city" (Prov. 16:32, *NASB*).
- "A man of *knowledge* uses words with restraint, and a man of *understanding* is even-tempered. Even a fool is thought wise if he keeps silent, and discerning if he holds his tongue" (Prov. 17:27-28).
- "A man's *discretion* makes his slow to anger. And it is his glory to overlook a transgression" (Prov. 19:11, *NASB*).

The point is clear. The more we understand *why* another person is responding in anger, the more we are able to control our own anger. Putting it in the language of today, when we develop objectivity there is less tendency to perceive anger as a personal attack on us; with this interpretation we are less threatened; and when we are less threatened we learn to control our emotions—and particularly the emotion we call anger.

So, let us be quick to listen—yes, to God's Word which teaches us many things, but particularly how to control anger. But let us also understand the *process*. When we listen carefully before we speak we'll find ourselves seeing things more objectively and we are less likely to respond emotionally. And when we take this approach we are much more likely to "bring about the righteous life that God desires" (Jas. 1:20).

A QUESTION TO THINK ABOUT

To what extent am I practicing James's secret to a successful life?

First, be quick to listen.

Second, be slow to speak.

Third, be slow to become angry.

The Echo

I shouted aloud and louder
While out on the plain one day;
The sound grew faint and fainter
Until it had died away.
My words had gone forever.
They left no trace or track,
But the hills nearby caught up the cry
And sent an echo back.

I spoke a word in anger
To one who was my friend,
Like a knife it cut him deeply,
A wound that was hard to mend.
That word, so thoughtlessly uttered,
I would we could both forget,
But its echo lives and memory gives
The recollection yet.

How many hearts are broken,
How many friends are lost
By some unkind word spoken
Before we count the cost!
But a word or deed of kindness
Will repay a hundredfold,
For it echoes again in the heart of men
And carries a joy untold.[1]

—C.A. Lufburrow

Note

1. C.A. Lufburrow, "The Echo," *Encyclopedia of Seven Thousand-Seven Hundred Illustrations: Signs of the Times.* (Rockville, MD: Assurance Publishers, 1979), p. 131.

9
What Must I Do to Live for Christ?

Therefore, get rid of all moral filth and the evil that is so prevalent, and humbly accept the word planted in you, which can save you (James 1:21).

The late Dr. J. Wilbur Chapman used to tell of a Methodist pastor who often spoke on the subject of sin. He minced no words, but defined sin as "that abominable thing God hates." A leader in his congregation on one occasion urged him to cease using the ugly word. Said he: "Dr. Howard, we wish you would not speak so plainly about sin. Our young people, hearing you, will be more likely to indulge in sin. Call it something else, an 'inhibition,' or 'error,' or 'mistake,' or even a 'twist in our nature.' "

"I understand what you mean," the pastor remarked, and going to his desk he brought out a little bottle. "This bottle," he said, "contains strychnine. You will see that the red label here reads 'poison.' Would you suggest that I change the label, and paste one on that says, 'wintergreen'? You see," he continued, "the more harmless the name, the more dangerous the dose will be."

James was also this kind of pastor. He pulled no punches when talking about sin. He didn't write what Christians *want* to hear. Rather he wrote what we *need* to hear. He spoke out plainly and pointedly about sin. He never watered down his message. So, as spiritual leaders today, can we do less if we're going to be true to the Scriptures?

In this next section of his letter, James, in his inimitable style, jolts his readers with two powerful exhortations. Though briefly and succinctly stated, they are explosive in terms of meaning.

"PUT OFF YOUR OLD SELF" (Ephesians 4:22)

"Therefore, get rid of all moral filth and the evil that is so prevalent" (Jas. 1:21). The continuity in James's thinking is very obvious. In the previous verse he warned against becoming angry, stating clearly that "man's *anger* does not bring about the *righteous life* God desires." And in view of this reality, James now exhorts his readers to, in essence, get rid of all unrighteous.

There is then a definite cause-effect relationship between anger and certain kinds of sin. James generalizes with such concepts as "unrighteousness," "moral filth," and "evil." But again Paul filled in James's broad outline with specific details. In a sense, James often gives us the main points relative to Christian living and Paul adds the subpoints.

What specific sins result when anger causes a Christian to resort to unrighteous attitudes and action?

Falsehood

In both of his letters, one to the Ephesians and the other to the Colossians, Paul referred to deceitfulness in the same context in which he dealt with anger. "Therefore," he wrote, "each of you must *put off falsehood* and *speak truthfully* . . . " (Eph. 4:25). He then wrote, "In your anger do not sin" (Eph. 4:26). When we are angry we are vulnerable in this area of our lives. We give the devil a foothold.

How does this happen? One of the most prevalent ways is that we are tempted to say things that are not true about people who have made us angry. This is the root cause of many rumors. What more convenient and successful way to get even?

This kind of unrighteousness can become very subtle and deceitful—particularly among Christians. In fact, we can "deceive ourselves" as James points out in the next verse (Jas. 1:22). For example, we may be very angry at someone because of what they've done to us. And while in that emotional state—having "let the sun go down" while we are "still angry"—we hear something negative about that person. At that moment we're tempted to be "quick to listen"—*but* to the wrong thing. Anger can actually cause us to hear what we *want* to hear. Unfortunately, what we *think* we hear is often far worse than what is really true. We then pass that information on to someone else—which may be a half-truth or, more specifically, a lie.

The problem is complicated even more when we rationalize and pass the information on as a "spiritual" or "prayer" concern. For example, we may discover ourselves saying, "I don't want you to tell anyone else about this, but so-and-so, etc." We then go on to describe some negative information. To top it off, we conclude with the pious statement, "Remember, just pray about it."

At that juncture the damage is done! This is the most

convenient way of all of starting a rumor. In the process we come out looking righteous rather than unrighteous.

Stealing

People lie for various reasons. Anger is certainly not the only cause. And the same is true of stealing. But anger also makes a Christian vulnerable to this sin.

How so? Stealing can become a means of retaliation. For example, you may feel abused or used by your employer. Down deep you're angry. If you express how you feel, it may threaten your job security. Consequently, you discover a way to get even. Your conscience won't let you take concrete objects that don't belong to you. However, you steal time. And whether you realize it or not, *time* is *money*. Paul wrote, "He who has been stealing must steal no longer, but must *work,* doing something useful with his own hands, that he may have something to share with those in need" (Eph. 4:28).

Unwholesome Talk

One of the most prevalent ways in which we sin when we are angry is with our tongue. That's why James warned his readers to "be quick to *listen,* slow to *speak* and slow to become *angry."* Some people express anger in very vulgar ways. This is a particular temptation for a man or woman who has had a foul mouth before becoming a Christian.

I find it difficult to identify with this problem since I did not develop a habit of expressing my anger with bad language even before I became a Christian (I had other ways). I do know Christians who have a very difficult time controlling this tendency when they get angry. They revert very quickly to their old habit patterns.

Paul is very specific in warning against this sin. "Do not let any unwholesome talk come out of your mouths."

He then gave a positive perspective, "But only what is helpful for building others up according to their needs" (Eph. 4:29). Paul made the cause-effect relationship between "anger" and "unrighteous speech" even more clear in his letter to the Colossians. "Now you must rid yourself of all such things as these: anger, rage, malice, slander, *and filthy language from your lips*" (Col. 3:8).

Think for a moment what we have done in our society with foul language. No longer only "locker room" talk, it is now blurted unashamedly from movie screens. In anger, people ask God to damn people. In vain, we use the name of the most wonderful Person in the universe—Jesus Christ! In our anger we assign people to a dung heap! And we defame one of the most wonderful gifts God has given us with every four-letter word we can think of.

A successful owner of fine horses once told his trainers: "I have never seen a good-mannered horse that was sworn at. It hurts the feelings of a sensitive animal, and I'll keep my word to discharge any man caught swearing within the hearing of any horse in this stable."

The application, of course, is clear. If this kind of verbal abuse hurts a horse, how much more so another human being?

"Well, that leaves me out," you say. "I certainly don't swear or use 'filthy language.' "

That's commendable! But have you ever heard an angry parent shout, "You stupid, dumb, idiotic kid! Don't you have any sense at all?"

There is, of course, more than one way to use our tongue to vent our anger. And statements like this certainly do not measure up to Paul's criteria that as a Christian I am to speak *only* what is helpful for *building others up* according to their needs, that it may benefit those who listen" (Eph. 4:29). In fact, the words we use are not as important as our tone of voice in causing emotional damage. To call a kid "dumb" or "stupid" in anger may be just as hurtful as if we used profanity.

This does not mean we shouldn't discipline our children when they need it. And it doesn't mean that we should wait until we have no negative emotions about the situation. That's unrealistic. What it does mean is that when we're angry at our children (which is not wrong in itself), we should not sin in the process.

I remember on one occasion when my son was around eight or nine years old. We were sitting at the kitchen table having dinner. He was having a delightful time clinking his spoon in his iced tea glass, totally oblivious to the fact that it was rather irritating, especially to me. I'd had a rather stressful day which made me more vulnerable to an emotional reaction.

However, I asked him to stop in a very calm voice. He did—for about thirty seconds, and then continued the process. And again, I asked him to stop—quite calmly. And again, he was responsive—for about fifteen seconds. And then he was at it again.

At that moment I had had enough. I turned to him, called his name, looked him straight in the eye and said (with a certain amount of emotion in my voice), "Kenton, what you're doing is making me angry. It irritates me! I've asked you to stop twice before. Now please stop!!!"

The expression on his face revealed that I had his attention. But then he surprised me. "Oh—okay, Dad," he replied in an understanding voice. "I won't do it again!" And he didn't.

You see, if there was one emotion he could identify with and understand, it was anger. And when he knew how I was feeling about the situation, he really heard me for the first time.

Anger per se—as we shared in the last chapter—is not sin. It is natural. But how we express that anger can become sin. And when we discipline our children or have to confront other situations, it is not wrong to let other people know we're angry. In fact, it may be helpful. But *what* we say and *how* we say it is very important. If we attack the person, put him down, or humiliate him, or accuse him falsely because of our own emotional reactions, we had better wait until we're in control. I find it a good policy in most situations, particularly when other adults are involved, to give myself at least twenty-four hours before I deal with problems that have made me angry. Usually, after waiting awhile, I actually see the situation quite differently. Though I may still have to confront the problem, I'm able to do so far more objectively.

Another suggestion: If possible, avoid dealing with people who make you angry when you're tired or not feeling well. Under these conditions we are far more vulnerable to subjective reactions we'll later regret. In this respect we must realize that Paul's statement to not let the sun go down while we're still angry does not mean we should never wait to deal with the circumstances that have made us angry. Rather, he is saying we should deal with our anger and not allow it to turn to bitterness. One way to deal with that anger is to get emotional distance on the problem before we confront it.

Sexual Immorality

Sexual immorality, of course, is always wrong, no matter what the cause. "But among you," Paul also wrote to the Ephesians, "there must not be even a hint of sexual immorality, or any kind of impurity" (Eph. 5:3).

There are various reasons why people indulge their sexual appetites illegitimately, just as there are various reasons people lie, steal, and use foul language. But more often than most of us realize, anger is at the root of this kind of improper behavior. Though James does not mention this kind of sin specifically when dealing with the relationship between anger and unrighteousness, he seems to allude to it quite clearly when he said, "Therefore, get rid of all *moral filth* and the *evil* that is so prevalent" (Jas. 1:21).

Why would anger cause a person to commit a sexual sin? For one reason, it is a means of retaliation that hurts another person very deeply. I remember talking one day with a woman who had committed adultery. It was obvious that the basic cause was *not* uncontrollable sexual lust. It was anger. She was retaliating because her husband had hurt her deeply. He too had been unfaithful. She was getting even. Unfortunately, she also hurt herself in the process.

That is often the way it is with anger. It causes us to do things that make our own problems worse. But somehow we gain sufficient satisfaction from hurting the other person that we don't stop to consider how it will intensify our own hurt.

This emotional phenomenon is sometimes seen among young people who have deep resentment towards their parents. I have personally counseled teenage girls who have gotten pregnant to get even with a father or mother. This, of course, represents the ultimate in retaliation that brings embarrassment and hurt, not only to the object of anger, but to the angry person herself.

Again, it must be emphasized that anger is not the only or even the main reason that people commit sexual sins. But it *is* a reason. And it is usually combined with other emotional needs—feelings of rejection, insecurity, and inferiority, as well as just plain natural desires. But that is why it can be such a dangerous motivation. That is why James warned, "Be . . . slow to become angry, for man's anger does not bring about the righteous life God desires" (Jas. 1:19-20).

"PUT ON THE NEW SELF"
(Ephesians 4:24)

"And humbly accept the word planted in you, which can save you" (Jas. 1:21).

At this point, James focuses on the key to living like Christ rather than the world. In fact, as we'll see, the key *is* Christ!

Earlier, James spoke of the beginning point of the Christian life when he wrote that God "chose to give us birth through the *word of truth*" (Jas. 1:18). At this juncture we were "born again" if we responded to God's invitation to receive Jesus Christ as our Saviour from sin. Now James teaches these believers—and us too—how to live for Christ. He wrote, "Humbly accept the *word* planted in you, which can save you" (Jas. 1:21).

The Word Planted in You

What does James mean by the "word of truth"? The meaning is two-fold. First, Jesus Christ Himself *is* the *Word of Truth*. John made this clear in his Gospel when he wrote, "In the beginning was the *Word* and . . . the *Word* became flesh and lived for a while among us" (John 1:1,14). And later Jesus Himself said, "I am . . . the *truth*" (John 14:6).

However, Jesus did more than come into this world and live *among us*. For all those who respond to His love He also comes to live *within us*. And thus James wrote—"Humbly accept the word planted *in you*."

Again, Paul becomes our commentator on this concept. Of his own life he wrote, "I have been crucified with Christ and I no longer live, but *Christ lives in me*" (Gal. 2:20). And writing to the Colossians he reminded them of that great and wonderful mystery "which is *Christ in you,* the hope of glory" (Col. 1:27).

I personally do not understand all that this means.

Consequently, I can't satisfactorily explain what it means. And that should not surprise us because Paul calls it a "mystery." I'm not sure he understood it clearly either.

But I know it's true. And if I humbly accept that fact and yield myself to the indwelling Christ, and at the same time turn my back on sin and evil, He will enable me to live a life pleasing to Him.

But, as with salvation, I must respond to His invitation. I must activate the process. I must "put off" the "old self"—to quote Paul, and "put on the new self, created to be like God in true righteousness and holiness" (Eph. 4:22,24). And it is Christ Himself who lives within us to enable us to conform our lives to His life.

But there's another dimension to James's statement. To "humbly accept the word planted in you" is more than a mystical concept that defies explanation. The meaning is very concrete and practical. He is referring to the "written word" which reveals the living Word. In fact, it is dangerous to divide these two concepts. If we talk merely about the living Word dwelling within us, we can become purely mystical and subjective in our Christian experience. In fact, we are vulnerable to misinterpreting our mental and emotional experiences and classifying them as being from God, whereas they may be purely from experiences that may even reflect carnal and illegitimate motives and appetites.

On the other hand, if we think only of the *written* Word of God we are in danger of making Christianity purely an academic experience that is basically cognitive and intellectual. We are in danger of losing the supernatural and mystical dimension of our faith.

When James wrote, "Humbly accept the word planted in you," I believe he was referring to both the living Word *and* the written word. In fact, the person of Christ in our lives becomes meaningless apart from what He taught.

Thus He told His disciples on one occasion that if they really loved Him and chose to remain or abide in Him, they would *obey His commands* (John 15:1-12). Abiding in Christ is not some kind of mystical experience that suddenly enables us to rise above the world's system and to live a victorious Christian life. The "abiding" is a very concrete experience. It means obeying Christ's word in conjunction with His indwelling presence. And this is what James had in mind.

Paul reflects that balance beautifully in his letter to the Colossians when he wrote, "Let the *word of Christ dwell in you richly* as you teach and admonish one another with all wisdom, and as you sing psalms, hymns and spiritual songs with gratitude in your hearts to God. And whatever you do, whether in word or deed, do it all in the name of the Lord Jesus, giving thanks to God the Father through him" (Col. 3:16-17).

Which Can Save You

It is the Word planted in us, humbly accepted, that can *save us*. At this point it is important to understand that the word *save*—as James uses it here in verse 21—does not refer to our eternal salvation. We have already been saved by responding to the Word when we are born again. Rather, James is referring to being saved or rescued from the *power* of sin. The Greek verb *coozoo* used here literally means "to preserve" or "to keep safe." In other words, it is the indwelling Word of God—both living and written—that protects our soul from "moral filth" and "evil" that surrounds us.

WHAT ABOUT YOU?

Have you considered how anger may be causing you to commit some of the specific sins alluded to by James and specified by Paul?

- Can you think of instances where you have been or are being *untruthful* because you are angry at someone?
- What about *stealing*? Are you taking what doesn't belong to you because someone has hurt you and made you angry?
- What about your *language*? Is it wholesome? Or are you venting your wrath with a bitter tongue?
- What about your *moral life*? Are you sinning against God, your family, your fellow Christians and the God you serve because you are bitter?

James tells us to deal with the root causes. "Be quick to listen, slow to speak and slow to become angry, for man's anger does not bring about the righteous life that God desires. Therefore, get rid of all moral filth and the evil that is so prevalent . . . " (Jas. 1:19-21).

Have you humbly accepted the word planted in you that can save you? As you deal with the root causes for anger and sin, claim God's promise that Christ dwells in your heart by faith. Recognize that His presence and power are activated by the written Word of God. Therefore, "do not merely listen to the word, and so deceive yourselves. Do what it says." But that's another chapter!

In conclusion I'm reminded of the story of the young person who asked a pastor a question. "You say that unsaved people carry a weight of sin. I feel nothing. How heavy is sin? Is it ten pounds? Eighty pounds?"

The pastor replied by asking the youth a question as well, "If you laid a 400-pound weight on a corpse, would it feel the load?"

The youth replied, "It would feel nothing, because it is dead."

The pastor concluded, "The spirit too is indeed dead which feels no load of sin or is indifferent to its burden and flippant about its presence." The young person was silenced!

It is possible, of course, for a Christian to harden his heart and conscience against sin. That, of course, is a very sad position for a Christian to get himself into. But maybe it's true that you have not been sensitive to sin because the Word has not been planted in you. You've not been born again. Spiritually you are dead.

You can correct that problem by confessing your sin, no matter how you *feel* about your sin, and by receiving Jesus Christ as your personal Saviour. The Bible says that "if we claim to be without sin, we deceive ourselves and the *truth* is not in us." Then John added:

"If we claim we have not sinned, we make him out to be a liar and his *word* has no place in our lives" (1 John 1:8,10).

However, in between these two straightforward verses, John also writes, "If we confess our sins, he is faithful and just and will forgive us our sins and purify us from all unrighteousness" (v. 9). That promise applies to both the Christian and the non-Christian.

What about you? Have you acknowledged your sins?

10
What Does God Expect from His Children?

Do not merely listen to the word, and so deceive yourselves. Do what it says. Anyone who listens to the word but does not do what it says is like a man who looks at his face in a mirror and, after looking at himself, goes away and immediately forgets what he looks like. But the man who looks intently into the perfect law that gives freedom, and continues to do this, not forgetting what he has heard, but doing it—he will be blessed in what he does (James 1:22-25).

A missionary translator was endeavoring to find a word for *obedience* in the native language. This was a virtue seldom practiced among the people into whose language he wanted to translate the New Testament. As he returned home from the village one day, he whistled for his dog and he came running at full speed. An old native, seeing this, said admiringly in the native tongue, "Your dog is all ear." Immediately the missionary knew he had his word for obedience.

James, more than any other New Testament writer, was concerned about obedience. He taught that a person who claims to be a Christian but disobeys God's laws is self-deceived. The word in the Greek literally means to reason incorrectly or to miscalculate.

AN OLD TESTAMENT EXAMPLE

God's Dealings with the Amalekites

After Saul became king of Israel, God spoke to him through the prophet Samuel and outlined very clearly and specifically what He was going to do to the Amalekites for what they had done to the children of Israel when they came up out of Egypt. The Israelites were in the midst of a strange wilderness without any kind of societal organization. They were without normal food and water supplies and without permanent housing. Furthermore, they had no trained army to protect themselves from their enemies. While in this vulnerable position, the Amalekites mercilessly attacked Israel at Rephidim. Though Israel may have been a threat, what the Amalekites did was a reflection of the wickedness and evil that had permeated their own culture for years.

God's wrath. Against impossible odds God helped Israel win a stunning supernatural victory over these people. But the Lord was so displeased with the Amalekites that He had Moses put in writing that He was going to eventually punish these people for their sins. "Write this on a scroll as something to be remembered," the Lord said to Moses, "and make sure that Joshua hears it, because I will *completely erase* the memory of the Amalekites from under heaven" (Exod. 17:14).

That day, God's judgment fell on these people. Though He had tolerated unbelievable sin, including child sacrifice and other abominable practices among these people, there came a time when His patience ran out and His anger was pushed to the point of judgment.

God's mercy. In many respects God was showing mercy when He allowed the children of these wicked people to be killed in infancy rather than allow them to grow up in a pagan environment, learning the evil ways of their parents and becoming adults who would be held accountable for their actions. It's my personal opinion that there will be many children in heaven whose lives God allowed to be taken in infancy to spare them the judgment of eternal separation from His presence, which they would have experienced had they lived to the age of accountability. As they grew and were exposed to the parents' sinful ways, their doom would have been sealed.

God's judgment. Nevertheless, God pronounced judgment on the Amalekites—and put it in writing! And when Saul became king of Israel, the Lord instructed him through the prophet Samuel to wipe these people off the face of the earth. "I will punish the Amalekites for what they did to Israel when they waylaid them as they came up from Egypt," the Lord said. "Now go, attack the Amalekites and *totally destroy everything that belongs to them.* Do not spare them; put to death men and women, children and infants, cattle and sheep, camels and donkeys" (1 Sam. 15:2-3).

God's patience. Note that God did not bring His judgment upon the Amalekites for a number of generations. The reason the Lord waited so long can be found in one word—*mercy.* God is long-suffering and does not want anyone to perish, as Peter reveals in his second epistle (2

Pet. 3:9). Even though God had put this judgment in writing He would not have hesitated to change His mind if they had repented, just as He did later when the wicked people of Nineveh listened to Jonah's proclamation of judgment. When God saw their repentance and that they had "turned from their evil ways, he had compassion and did not bring upon them the destruction he had threatened" (Jon. 3:10).

God's Instructions to Saul

Even many generations later after they had seen the great and mighty deeds God did for Israel, including His mighty revelations from Mount Sinai and His subsequent judgments upon Israel when they disobeyed His laws, there was not repentance among the Amalekites. Consequently, God's judgment fell, as it always does when there is no response to long-suffering and grace. Saul, as the first king of Israel, was to be the human agent to bring about this judgment.

Saul's disobedience. Saul *disobeyed* God. He "spared Agag" the Amalekite king, as well as "the best of the sheep and cattle, and fat calves and lambs—everything that was good" (1 Sam. 15:9). And the Lord was very displeased. In fact, He expressed His displeasure to Samuel, saying, "I am grieved that I have made Saul king, because he has turned away from me and has not carried out my instructions" (1 Sam. 15:11).

On the surface it may appear that Saul made an innocent mistake. However, he was motivated by rebellion and pride. He revealed his arrogance by going to Carmel and setting "up a monument in his own honor" (1 Sam. 15:12). Samuel later charged him with a rebellious spirit (1 Sam. 15:23), which is always at the root of disobedience.

Samuel's confrontation and Saul's rationalization. When Samuel arrived on the scene to convey to Saul God's message of displeasure, Saul greeted him with an air of innocence. "The Lord bless you!" he called out to Samuel. "I have carried out the Lord's instructions" (1 Sam. 15:13).

But Samuel immediately went to the heart of the matter. In the background he could hear the "bleating of sheep" and the "lowing of cattle" (1 Sam. 15:14). "What is this?" he asked Saul. The king's response was typical of those of us who disobey God but work out in our own minds an acceptable rationalization for our behavior. First he shifted the burden of responsibility to someone else— in this case, his men. "*Soldiers* brought them from the Amalekites," he told Samuel. But in doing so he also defended their actions, primarily because their actions were his own. "They spared the best of the sheep and cattle to sacrifice to the Lord your God, but," he hurriedly continued, "we totally destroyed the rest" (1 Sam. 15:15). Saul's response had all the earmarks of a guilty conscience.

Because of God's direct revelation to him, plus the obvious evidence that Saul was wrong, Samuel discerned clearly what Saul was up to. He abruptly interrupted his story. "Stop!" he said. "Let me tell you what the Lord said to me last night" (1 Sam. 15:16).

Again Samuel did not skirt the issue. Pride was at the root of Saul's disobedience. Before God had anointed him as king of Israel, Saul's view of himself was one of unworthiness and humility. Though he was "an impressive young man without equal among the Israelites" (he was "a head taller than any of the others") (1 Sam. 9:2), he did not understand why God favored him with such a high calling.

But position and power went to Saul's head. He was self-deceived. He began to attribute his success as king of Israel to his own abilities and took to himself honor that belonged to God. In the process of fulfilling the will of God, he decided to depart from the Lord's clear instructions. He did not destroy everything among the Amalekites as God had clearly specified.

"Why did you not obey the Lord?" Samuel asked (1 Sam. 15:19). At this point Saul repeated his rationalization, stating that the soldiers' motivation was to keep the best of the animals to sacrifice to God (1 Sam. 15:21).

Samuel's response was direct, convicting, and very painful for Saul. "To obey is better than sacrifice, and to heed is better than the fat of rams. For *rebellion* is like the sin of divination, and *arrogance* like the evil of idolatry" (1 Sam. 15:22-23).

With this statement, Samuel unveiled Saul's problem. Saul's pride had led to deliberate rebellion against the Lord. And because of the seriousness of this sin and his high position in Israel, God rejected him as king (1 Sam. 15:23). Though Saul reigned many years after that event, he did so without God's blessing.

Saul's persistent rebellion and tragic ending. It's important to point out at this juncture that God did not reject Saul as a man. He rejected his position. Saul had many opportunities to accept this verdict and to humble himself before God and to receive God's blessing in a lesser role. But jealousy, anger, and intense depression became a persistent part of his life. He rejected the opportunities God gave him to soften his heart. He never accepted the fact that God was going to replace him with another man to reign as king. This pride, jealousy, and anger eventually led him to dabble in witchcraft (1 Sam. 28:7), and eventually he committed suicide (1 Sam. 31:4).

JESUS' ILLUSTRATION

On one occasion Jesus used a graphic illustration to underscore the importance of obedience, as well as the seriousness of disobedience. He focused the problem with a question—"Why do you call me 'Lord, Lord,' and do not do what I say?" (Luke 6:46).

Inherent in this question is a contradiction. It is inconsistent for any Christian to call Jesus "Lord" if he is disobedient. The term *Lord* implies obedience and submission. As someone has said, "If Jesus is not Lord *of all,* He's not Lord *at all.*"

The House That Stood and the House That Fell

Jesus then used an illustration—as He often did—to get His point across. "I will show you," He said, "what he is like who comes to me and *hears my words* and *puts them into practice*" (Luke 6:47). He then told the story of a man who built a house. He "dug down deep and laid the foundation on rock." Then a severe storm descended on his house. But it withstood the wind and the rain because it had a solid footing (6:48).

Another man built a house, but he did not prepare the foundation. He simply built the structure from the ground up. And when a violent storm came, the ground eroded and the building collapsed. "Its destruction," Jesus said, "was complete" (6:49).

With this story, Jesus did not leave the application to the listeners' imagination. "The one who hears my words," He said, "and *does not put them into practice* is like a man who built a house on the ground without a foundation." His life will eventually collapse and if he doesn't take corrective measures, the destruction will be beyond repair.

Saul's Experience and Jesus' Illustration

Saul's life illustrates what Jesus was teaching in the ultimate sense. Fortunately, not all disobedience leads to such serious consequences. As pointed out earlier, even in Saul's case, God would have responded to Saul's repentance. Had he accepted the natural consequences of his sin, the Lord, as always, would have blessed him in a lesser capacity. But he never really humbled himself before God. Rather, he tried to prove God wrong—which is the height of arrogance. And eventually his "house" collapsed completely. Sadly, "its destruction was complete."

These are sobering illustrations. And that is why James said, "Do not merely listen to the word, and *so deceive yourselves.* Do what it says" (Jas. 1:22). Saul was deceived. He rationalized his behavior and then blamed others. And the root of his self-deception was pride. It led to rebellion, subtle though it was.

And note also that his disobedience was not total but partial. This made the problem of self-deception and rationalization even more insidious. After all, he reasoned, he was disobeying God in order to honor and worship God. At this moment in Saul's mind the end justified the means. And that kind of reasoning always leads to serious consequences.

JAMES'S ILLUSTRATION

James used an illustration of his own to make his point. "Anyone who listens to the word but does not do what it says is like a man who looks at his face in a mirror and, after looking at himself, goes away and immediately forgets what he looks like" (Jas. 1:23-24).

All of us can identify with this illustration. We've all looked in a mirror. In fact, we probably engage in this activity more times a day than most any other single activity. The mirror reflects our physical image. It shows us what we look like. And it does not lie. When I see an unshaven face or disheveled hair, it is a reality. I can pick up a razor and shave and brush my hair and correct the problem. Or I can walk away and go through the day in an unkempt state, literally forgetting how I look to others.

That kind of behavior, James wrote, is like the man

who is exposed to God's Word, sees those things that need correcting, turns away and immediately forgets that his spiritual image is not in harmony with what God desires.

On the other hand, James wrote about a Christian who "looks intently into the perfect law that gives freedom, and continues to do this, not forgetting what he has heard, but doing it—he will be blessed in what he does" (Jas. 1:25).

Note two things in this illustration. First, obedience to God's Word brings *freedom*. Secondly, obedience brings *blessing*.

Obedience Brings Freedom

There are many Christians who believe that if they obey God they will be brought into bondage. They fear that they'll not be able to enjoy life. This, in itself, is self-deception. This kind of thinking is reflective of what happened to Eve in the Garden of Eden when she was deceived by Satan. His strategy was to convince Eve that she would not experience a full life of knowledge and wisdom if she obeyed God's command to refrain from eating of the fruit of the tree in the midst of the garden. She succumbed to temptation and disobeyed God. Adam too disobeyed—and together they brought the whole world into bondage.

Obeying God brings freedom, not bondage. Conversely, disobedience destroys freedom.

Sin is a hard taskmaster. Once we are in its grip we become enslaved. And there is nothing so imprisoning than to be associated with other people who are also slaves to sin. Because we are social creatures, we then become a slave to their sins as well. And we find ourselves enslaving others. In short, we are used by others for their own selfish ends and we use others in the same way.

Paul wrote about this freedom in his letter to the Galatians. "You, my brothers, were called to be free. But do not use your freedom to indulge the sinful nature; rather, serve one another in love" (Gal. 5:13).

There are two kinds of slavery. One is to be a servant of sin itself. The other is to be a servant of God and others in the context of the will of God. Contradictory as it sounds, the latter kind of servanthood bring true freedom. This is what Jesus meant when He said that he who loses his life will find it again.

James, then, tells us that if we "look intently into the perfect law"—God's Word—not only listening to what it says, but doing what it says, we will find true freedom.

Obedience Brings Blessing

Obeying God not only sets us free, it also brings blessing. God's words to Joshua illustrate this point. "Be careful *to obey* all the law my servant Moses gave you; do not turn from it to the right or to the left. . . . Do not let this Book of the Law depart from your mouth; meditate on it day and night, so that you may be careful to do everything written in it. Then," God told Joshua, "you will be *prosperous* and *successful*" (Josh. 1:7-8).

God honors obedience. This is His promise. This does not mean, however, there will never be problems or difficulties in our lives because we stand for what is right and true. "In fact," the Scriptures say clearly that "everyone who wants to live a godly life in Christ Jesus will be persecuted" (2 Tim. 3:12). But ultimately, God will bless us for obeying what He says. Let me illustrate.

I know a man and his wife who accepted a position in a church as one of the pastoral associates. On the surface, when the invitation came to accept this position, everything looked wonderful. Consequently he resigned from a very successful position in one church and moved his family across the country to take this new ministry.

However, very soon, this young couple began to sense something was wrong in the church. For one thing, what was being taught from the pulpit didn't sound right. Often it was not so much what was said, but the way it was said. In addition, the pastor's behavior didn't seem to coincide with his own teaching. And his wife's behavior was even more inconsistent.

Sensing something was seriously wrong, this new associate eventually confronted the pastor and his wife with their inconsistent behavior. As a result, he was immediately accused of insubordination and the pastor convinced the elders to remove the assistant from his position. The pastor also publicly forbade everyone in the church to talk to the dismissed pastor and his wife, and even warned his people that their children should not talk to the children of the couple dismissed from the church staff. In other words, this little family was cut off completely from the church and from any spiritual or social fellowship. And since they were relatively new in that part of the country, they had no one to turn to for immediate fellowship and support. Needless to say, the feelings of alienation and emotional pain were excruciating.

Two major things happened after these events. The wife of the man who had been dismissed contracted cancer. Though it certainly cannot be proved, some actually believed that it was the deep emotional pain and stress she experienced, because of these events, that triggered the cancer. Some believe that cancer strikes in areas that are physically weak and vulnerable to stress. Nevertheless, she died thirteen months later at age thirty-nine.

But something happened before she died. Several months after the dismissal, one of the women in the church where this couple had served—a wife of one of the elders—could stand the guilt no longer. She confessed to her husband and the congregation that she had been having an affair with the pastor, the very man who had dismissed the other man for confronting him with his own sins. Shortly, another elder's wife confessed.

The people who had followed this man's leadership were, of course, dumbfounded and horrified. The pastor was ultimately dismissed and some of the people did all they could to make things right with the young man and his wife—particularly before she died.

I spent many hours with this man and his teenage children and I am absolutely amazed at God's grace in their lives. Even in the midst of their deep emotional pain and hurt, he referred to the passages of Scripture that state clearly that obedience brings blessing. Yes, he paid a great price for taking a stand against sin—even if there is no connection between his wife's terminal illness and the events. He was falsely accused, dismissed from his position, and his little family was isolated and cut off socially. But he is convinced that God will not renege on His promises to bring ultimate blessing on his life and his children's lives—far beyond anything they've ever experienced before. And, already I have begun to see those blessings unfold.

James wrote "But the man who looks intently into the perfect law that gives freedom, and continues to do this, not forgetting what he has heard, but doing it—he *will be blessed in what he does.*"

WHAT ABOUT YOU?

Part of Satan's deception is to try to convince us that this principle is not true. He tells us that if we follow our own selfish desires, we'll be better off. This is exactly what happened to Adam and Eve in the Garden of Eden.

"Don't be deceived!" James wrote (Jas. 1:16; also v. 22). Though there may be immediate problems and pain, the ultimate results of obedience will far outweigh the price we have to pay initially. God *is* faithful!

HAVE YOU MADE JESUS CHRIST LORD OF YOUR LIFE?

First, have you become His follower? Have you become a Christian? There is no way we can obey Christ's teachings without first of all inviting Him to be our Saviour from sin. Then and only then can we experience the freedom and the blessings James wrote about. Remember, he was writing to those who had already become Christians.

Listen to the apostle Paul, who makes this point very clear: "Therefore, there is now no condemnation for those who are in Christ Jesus, because through Christ Jesus the law of the Spirit of life set me *free* from the law of sin and death. For what the law was powerless to do in that it was weakened by the sinful nature, God did by sending his own Son in the likeness of sinful man to be a sin offering. And so he condemned sin in sinful man, in order that the righteous requirements of the law might be fully met in us, who do not live according to the sinful nature but according to the spirit" (Rom. 8:1-4).

So, to experience freedom in Christ, you must obey Christ who said, "Whoever believes in the Son has eternal life, but whoever rejects the Son will not see life, for God's wrath remains on him" (John 3:36).

Second, what about your Christian experience? Since you have become a Christian, are you obeying Christ? Remember that Jesus said, "If anyone loves me, he will *obey* my teaching. My Father will love him, and we will come to him and make our home with him. He who does not love me will *not obey* my teaching" (John 14:23-24).

Following are areas where we are to obey Christ as a Christian, and if we do, God promises blessing. Evaluate your own life:

• *Serving others:*

In the context of washing the disciples' feet, Jesus admonished them to serve others as He had served them. Then He said, "Now that you know these things, you will be *blessed* if you do them" (John 13:17).

- *Responding to persecution with love:*
Peter wrote: "Do not repay evil with evil or insult with insult, but with blessing, because to this you were called so that you may *inherit a blessing*" (1 Pet. 3:9).

- *Being a good steward of our material resources:*
Malachi wrote, " 'Bring the whole tithe into the storehouse, that there may be food in my house. Test me in this,' says the Lord Almighty, 'and see if I will not throw open the floodgates of heaven and pour out so much *blessing* that you will not have room enough for it' " (Mal. 3:10). Paul wrote: "Remember this: Whoever sows sparingly will also reap sparingly, and whoever sows generously will also reap generously" (2 Cor. 9:6).

- *Living a godly and holy life:*
Solomon wrote: "*Blessings* crown the head of the righteous" (Prov. 10:6). David wrote: "Who may ascend the hill of the Lord? Who may stand in his holy place? He who has clean hands and a pure heart, who does not lift up his soul to an idol or swear by what is false. He will receive *blessing* from the Lord" (Ps. 24:3-5).

11
What Is a Christian's Greatest Asset and Greatest Liability?

If anyone considers himself religious and yet does not keep a tight rein on his tongue, he deceives himself and his religion is worthless (James 1:26).

What is a Christian's greatest asset, and his greatest liability? The answer to this question is very clear in the book of James. On the negative side, James states, "If anyone considers himself to be religious and yet does not keep a tight rein on his tongue, he deceives himself and his religion is worthless" (Jas. 1:26). Later, he states the positive side, "If anyone is never at fault in what he says, he is a perfect man, able to keep his whole body in check" (Jas. 3:2).

A CHRISTIAN'S GREATEST LIABILITY

There are various measurements which can be used to evaluate the depth of our Christian experience. But none is so comprehensive and revealing as how we use our tongue.

This is understandable. According to statisticians, the average person spends at least one-fifth of his or her life talking. Ordinarily, in a single day enough words are used to fill a fifty-page book. In one year's time, the average person's words would fill 132 books, each containing 400 pages.

Or, according to another statistician, the average person spends at least thirteen years of his life talking. On a normal day, he is likely to speak something like 18,000 words, roughly equivalent to a book of fifty-four pages. And in the course of a single year, his words would fill sixty-six books, each containing 800 pages.

It should not surprise us then that how we use our tongue reveals so much about us. It is the natural means whereby we demonstrate what we really are. Someone has said that people would perhaps be fortunate to be like crocodiles—at least in one respect. Crocodiles have a jaw, lips, and teeth, but no tongue. We might go on to say that a crocodile can bite, but he has to come in contact with his victim. With my tongue I could literally destroy another person's reputation and not even communicate face to face.

James uses a similar illustration to get his point across. He warns a Christian to "keep a tight *rein* on his tongue" (1:26).

If you have ever ridden a horse you know how important it is to keep a "tight rein," especially if you're riding a spunky, energetic animal. When I was a young kid back on the farm in Indiana, my dad bought me a beautiful roan. His name was Marvel. In many respects he was far more horse than a young kid could handle. He was five gaited, would rear at the slightest provocation, and had been well trained for roping cattle. The moment you hit the saddle he was off like greased lightning, and the moment you leaned to dismount, he'd plant his feet and slide to a screeching halt. Actually, my dad didn't know what kind of horse he was buying. And neither did I, since I had never ridden before. Believe me, Marvel and I learned a lot together.

The first thing my dad did was to replace the leather strap on the bridle with a chain. As a young boy, I didn't have enough grip and strength to be able to control the horse. The chain helped.

But that still didn't solve all my problems. I remember one day as if it were yesterday; it still sends chills up and down my spine. I was riding on the side of a busy highway. I had a rather loose grip on the reins, riding along casually, no doubt thinking about something else. Suddenly—and to this day I don't know what happened—something spooked old Marvel. Before I knew what happened, he shot sideways across the highway right in front of a speeding car. We were both within seconds of being hit. It happened so quickly that it was over before I had opportunity to be frightened. In retrospect, however, I could still break out in a cold sweat if I thought about the event too long.

Perhaps this personal story helps us understand more fully why James uses this kind of illustration to help us see the importance of keeping a "tight rein" on our tongues. If we don't, they can easily get out of control.

James elaborates even more in chapter 3 and supplements his first example with additional illustrations. We read, "When we put bits in the mouths of horses to make them obey us, we can turn the whole animal. Or take ships as an example. Although they are so large and are driven by strong winds, they are steered by a very small rudder wherever the pilot wants to go."

At this point James applies the illustration. "Likewise," he continues, "the tongue is a small part of the body, but it makes great boasts" (Jas. 3:3-5).

James then uses a third illustration, which in itself is significant. Ordinarily, one illustration helps get a point across. Why three? The answer, of course, is that James is dealing with a very important concept. He wants our attention. Thus, he continues, "Consider what a great forest is set on fire by a small spark" (Jas. 3:5). Today we might say, "Consider how a beautiful forest preserve can be literally destroyed by one cigarette butt carelessly thrown on the ground, or consider how large sections of a national park can be wiped out by one live coal left from a small campfire." And once the damage is done, it takes years to replace that beautiful forest. And so it is with a reputation that has been hurt by a loose tongue.

James again makes the application, "The tongue also is a fire, a world of evil among the parts of the body. It corrupts the whole person, sets the whole course of his life on fire, and is itself set on fire by hell" (Jas. 3:6).

These are strong words. But keep in mind that they are the words of God. James is not exaggerating with some kind of hyperbolic examples.

Paul also had a great deal to say about problems caused by our tongues. The word he used to describe malicious talk, gossip, and slandering in his second letter to Timothy and his letter to Titus (2 Tim. 3:3; Titus 2:3) is in essence the word used for "Satan" or "devil" in the New Testament. The correlation, of course, is clear. Satan has been a slanderer and false accuser ever since he fell from his place of glory and honor in heaven. "There is no truth in him," Jesus said. "When he lies, he speaks his native language, for he is a liar and the father of lies" (John 8:44).

Satan is the root of *all evil*. And since the tongue is

capable of great evil, the ultimate source of that evil is Satan himself, with enormous power over mankind. Thus James added, "All kinds of animals, birds, reptiles and creatures of the sea are being tamed and have been tamed by man, but no man can tame the tongue. It is a restless evil, full of deadly poison" (Jas. 3:7-8).

A CHRISTIAN'S GREATEST ASSET

As is so often true, a person's greatest weakness can also be his greatest strength. So it is with the tongue. Though we are capable of inflicting great hurt upon others with this great gift God gave us, we can also use it to bring great healing to men's hearts. No Christian, of course, is perfect. We can never achieve God's standard of righteousness in a complete sense while on this earth. James underscored this reality when he wrote, "We all stumble in many ways." But he also made another strong point. Continuing the thought he said, "If anyone is never at fault in what he says, he is a perfect man, able to keep his whole body in check" (Jas. 3:2).

The word in the Greek New Testament which is often translated "perfect" has at least two meanings. It can refer to ultimate perfection—when we are with Christ—or it can refer to a state of Christian maturity, even while on this earth. Here James may be referring to both meanings. On the one hand, a person who has complete control of his tongue might be considered perfect—which shows the power of the tongue. On the other hand, even a person who controls his tongue often has imperfect thoughts. Thus James's most practical point for us is that, as a Christian, even though I'm not perfect, if I'm able to control my tongue, I am in the process of reaching the kind of Christian maturity that is pleasing to Jesus Christ and admired by my friends and associates.

Note, too, that no one can control his tongue in his

own strength. James makes this point clear as well. "No man can tame the tongue," he wrote.

But there is a way. Paul wrote, "I can do everything through him who gives me strength" (Phil. 4:13). This is why we need Christ as our Saviour from sin—not only to inherit eternal salvation, but to be saved from the power of sin in this life. We must begin with the new birth James has already referred to earlier (Jas. 1:18). There's no way we can, in our own strength, be "quick to listen" and "slow to speak." And there is no way we can get beyond just listening to God's word in order to "do what it says" without God's help.

However, as James reminds us again and again, we must obey Christ. Deliverance from these problems is not automatic. We must bear final responsibility for our actions. And when we do, God will help us control our tongues. And the place to start is with new life in Christ. We must be changed from the inside out. This is what Jesus meant when He said, "What comes out of man is what makes him 'unclean.'" And on another occasion He said, "For out of the overflow of the heart the mouth speaks" (Matt. 12:34). This is why Paul exhorted every Christian to "take captive every thought to make it obedient to Christ" (2 Cor. 10:5).

James's point then is well made. When he said "If anyone considers himself religious and yet does not keep a tight rein on his tongue, he deceives himself and his religion is worthless" (Jas. 1:26). We are simply fooling ourselves. We are deceived. This is an inconsistency that should not be, which prompted James to later write— "With the tongue we praise our Lord and Father, and with it we curse men, who have been made in God's likeness. Out of the same mouth come praise and cursing. My brothers," he continued, "this should not be. Can both fresh water and salt water flow from the same spring? My brothers, can a fig tree bear olives, or a grapevine bear figs? Neither can a salt spring produce fresh water" (Jas. 3:9-12).

With these statements and questions, James is forcing his readers to evaluate their Christian experience. Note he graciously calls them "brothers." But he is raising a question, "If you *are* a Christian like you say you are, how can this be?" He then very wisely leaves the answer up to them.

WHAT ABOUT YOU?

James was not only speaking to first-century Christians. He was speaking to all of us as well. Though he no longer lives on this earth, his words still ring loud and clear because they are the words of God.

God has given us a great gift—a tongue. We have the potential to use it for good or evil. It can be our greatest asset or our greatest liability.

A number of Proverbs capture both dimensions. Listen to the Scriptures:

• "The tongue of the righteous is choice silver, but the heart of the wicked is of little value" (Prov. 10:20).
• "The lips of the righteous know what is fitting, but the mouth of the wicked only what is perverse" (Prov. 10:32).
• "Reckless words pierce like a sword, but the tongue of the wise brings healing" (Prov. 12:18).
• "Truthful lips endure forever, but a lying tongue lasts only a moment" (Prov. 12:19).
• "The tongue of the wise commends knowledge, but the mouth of the fool gushes folly" (Prov. 15:2).
• "The tongue that brings healing is a tree of life, but a deceitful tongue crushes the spirit" (Prov. 15:4).
• "The tongue has the power of life and death, and those who love it will eat its fruit" (Prov. 18:21).

A PERSONAL CHALLENGE

The Proverbs also tell us what happens when we use our tongue to help others rather than to hurt them. Listen to the following: "An anxious heart weighs a man down, but a kind word cheers him up" (Prov. 12:25).

At times all of us have experienced the kind of anxiety spoken about in this Proverb. It's that heavy feeling that comes over us when we're deeply troubled about something. It may be caused by family illness or the death of a close friend or relative. We might be disappointed in ourselves. We may have inadvertently hurt someone's feelings or let someone down. We may have failed to achieve some goal that was important to us. Or we may be disappointed in someone else who has let us down.

In Proverbs 12:25, Solomon is referring to the effects of a heavy heart. But, he also shares with us how that anxiety and heaviness can be dissipated. A *kind* word can cheer us up. To what extent are you healing broken hearts? You can! "Pleasant words are a honeycomb, sweet to the soul and healing to the bones" (Prov. 16:24).

Here Solomon equates pleasant words to the sweetness of honey. This is a beautiful analogy. Most of us know how pleasant it is to eat sweet things.

But notice the effect of pleasant words. They are "sweet to the *soul* and healing to the *bones.*" Man is basically a two-dimensional creature—both soul/spirit and body. To put it another way, we are both psychological beings and physical beings. And, of course, both are interrelated, so much so that we often talk about experiencing "psychosomatic" conditions. The first part of this word, *psycho,* comes from the Greek word *psyche,* meaning soul. The second part of the word, *somatic,* comes from the Greek word *soma,* meaning body. Therefore, psychosomatic refers to both the soul and body. Solomon reminds us that pleasant words affect both our psychological and physiological being in positive ways.

"A word aptly spoken is like apples of gold in settings of silver" (Prov. 25:11). This Proverb demonstrates the importance of choosing words carefully and sharing them at the right time. When we do, those words will never be forgotten.

I remember a specific incident that happened when I was in the first grade. The teacher, Olive Owens, had outlined the word *me* in a beautiful cursive style on the chalkboard. She then told us to copy the word on our papers.

I had never written a single *letter* in my life, let alone a *word*. Those were pre-"Sesame Street" days! Try as I might, I couldn't get my pencil to cooperate.

To my dismay, Miss Owens began to look at each student's work—one by one. I was in the third row of seats. She completed row one, came up row two, and then started down row three. My heart was pounding. What would she think of my inability? What would she do? These were pressing questions in my six-year-old heart.

And there she was, looking straight down at my paper and a few marks that resembled more a runaway seismograph than the efforts of a six-year-old boy. My heart was pounding even more and I was so overwhelmed with fear that I broke into tears.

At that moment Miss Owens did something that I'll never forget. She leaned over, and with a compassionate voice said, "That's all right, Gene." Then she sealed her words with a gentle kiss on my cheek.

To this day I remember that wonderful moment. It dispelled my fears and gave me courage to try again. I'm convinced that my teacher's gentle words helped me to take a giant step in the direction of liking school, rather than hating it.

Yes, the tongue is a small member of the body, but it is powerful for good or evil. Sometimes we do not use it for evil, but unfortunately, neither do we use it for good.

LIFE RESPONSE

Do you consider yourself to be religious and yet do not keep a tight rein on your tongue? If so, James said you have deceived yourself and your "religion is worthless."

Does this mean you are not a Christian? It could, but not necessarily. It is possible to be a true believer and yet fail God in this area. But James is saying that the impact of our lives on others may be meaningless.

Paul captured this reality in his letter to the Corinthians—men and women who were definitely Christians, but who lived very carnal and sinful lives. Thus he wrote:

• "If I speak in the tongues of men and of angels, but have not love, *I am only a resounding gong or a clanging* cymbal" (1 Cor. 13:1).

• "If I have the gift of prophecy and can fathom all mysteries and all knowledge, and if I have a faith that can move mountains, but have not love, *I am nothing*" (13:2).

• "If I give all I possess to the poor and surrender my body to the flames, but have not love, *I gain nothing*" (13:3).

THOUGHTS FOR MEDITATION

> One little unshed raindrop
> May think itself too small;
> Yet, somewhere a thirsty flower
>   Awaits its fall
>
> One little word, spoken,
> May seem too small to say;
> But, somewhere, for that word
>   A heart may pray.
>
> Helen Allison[1]

A careless word may kindle strife.
A cruel word may wreck a life,
A bitter word may hate instill;
A brutal word may smite and kill;

A gracious word may smooth the way;
A joyous word may light the day.
A timely word may lessen the stress;
A loving word may heal and bless.

Anonymous[2]

A PRAYER

Father, help me to use my tongue to bring healing and encouragement into other people's lives.
• Help me keep a tight rein on my tongue when I'm tempted to hurt another person.
• Help me to speak words of kindness.
• And when I *must* confront another, help me to always speak the truth in love.

Notes
1.*Encyclopedia of Seven Thousand-Seven Hundred Illustrations: Signs of the Times.* (Rockville, MD: Assurance Publishing, 1979), p. 1421.
2. Ibid.

12
What Kind of Religion Does God Accept?—Part I

Religion that God our Father accepts as pure and faultless is this: to look after orphans and widows in their distress and to keep oneself from being polluted by the world (James 1:27).

The word *religious* or *religion* is a word that confuses many people. Most people who use it to describe their experience or another person's experience usually believe that if their good works outweigh their bad works they'll eventually make it to heaven. In other words, people who believe in some kind of Supreme Being and who concentrate on doing good things are frequently referred to as "being religious."

This is certainly not what James had in mind. Rather, he used the word *religion* to describe a person's service to

God and others *as a Christian.* Thus a person who has accepted Christ as personal Saviour and who is conforming his life to Christ is living a religious life in the true sense of the word. That is what sets those involved in the "Christian religion" apart from those who follow other forms of religious philosophy.

How then do we recognize *true* religion? More specifically, what really pleases God about His children? What is a true reflection of our love for Jesus Christ? To watch and listen to some Christians, you might get the impression it is how consistently we share the gospel with those who don't know Him. Or, some seem to believe it is how often we go to church, or how much we read our Bibles and pray. Still others believe it is whether or not we are serving the Lord in full-time ministry—such as pastoring a church or serving as a foreign missionary.

No one would deny that all of these activities may be important reflections of our love for Christ. We *are* to share Christ with others (Matt. 28:19-20). And certainly we should not "give up meeting together, as some are in the habit of doing" (Heb. 10:25). Bible reading and prayer are also important exercises for every sincere Christian (2 Tim. 2:15; Col. 4:2). And those who serve the Lord in a full-time ministry should certainly be living dedicated Christian lives.

James tells us there is something more basic that reflects the depth of our love for God and His Son, Jesus Christ. "Religion that God our Father accepts as pure and faultless is this," James wrote; "to look after orphans and widows in their distress and to keep oneself from being polluted by the world" (Jas. 1:27). This chapter deals with the first of these priorities—"*to look after widows and orphans in their distress.*"

In some respects, these are rather unfamiliar words in our twentieth-century culture. But they were not unfamiliar in Old Testament and New Testament cultures. Before looking at what James is saying to us *today*, it's important to understand this biblical perspective.

THE OLD TESTAMENT CULTURE

In preparing His chosen people to enter the Promised Land, God once again spoke through Moses and carefully reviewed the Law He had given them in the wilderness on Mount Sinai. When they had first come out of Egypt, God made a couple of points very clear, which are recorded in the book of Exodus. The first involved the relationship with "aliens" or "strangers" that they would meet in their new environment. "Do not mistreat an *alien* or oppress him," God said, "for you were *aliens* in Egypt" (Exod. 22:21). In other words, God reminded them of their years of slavery and bondage in a foreign land and warned them not to treat others the way they had been treated.

Second, God was very specific regarding their attitudes and actions towards women without husbands and children without parents. "Do not take advantage of a *widow* or an *orphan*," God continued. "If you do and they cry out to me, I will certainly hear their cry" (Exod. 22:22-23).

In order to underscore the seriousness of this offense, and the depth of His own concern for these people, God outlined very specifically what would happen if they disobeyed Him in this matter. "My anger will be aroused," God said, "and I will kill you with the sword; *your* wives will become widows and *your* children fatherless" (Exod. 22:24). In other words, God warned them that their own family members would become victims of the same plight if they mistreated others.

After the wilderness wanderings, and just before the children of Israel were to enter Canaan, God reviewed these points from His Law with some elaboration. The extent of His concern is clear also from the number of times these warnings were repeated in the book of Deuteronomy:

"For the Lord your God . . . defends the cause of the *fatherless* and the *widow,* and loves the *alien,* giving him food and clothing. And you are to love those who are *aliens,* for you yourselves were *aliens* in Egypt" (Deut. 10:17-19).

Though God had chosen Israel for a specific purpose— to reveal His love to all mankind—He was not a God who was given to partiality. He loves all mankind. And for Israel to neglect these needy people would be to use God's grace in their own lives selfishly.

"At the end of every three years, bring all the tithes of that year's produce and store it in your towns, so that the *Levites* (who have no allotment or inheritance of their own) and the *aliens,* the *fatherless* and the *widows* who live in your towns may come and eat and be satisfied, and so that the Lord your God may bless you in all the work of your hands" (Deut. 14:28-29).

Here the Lord became more specific. Every third year the children of Israel were to lay aside one-tenth of their produce to care for the Levites. These people were chosen by God to preserve God's law, to see that it was obeyed, and to dispense justice where the law was disobeyed (Lev. 10:11; Deut. 17:18; 31:9-13; 33:8,10). They had no inheritance of their own in the land of Canaan, but lived in various cities throughout the land designated by the Lord.

Note however, that this third tithe every three years was to also provide for the "aliens, the fatherless and the widows." Note too that God's blessing upon Israel was dependent upon whether or not they provided for these people.

"Do not deprive the *alien* or the *fatherless* of justice, or take the cloak of the *widow* as a pledge. Remember that you were slaves in Egypt and the Lord your God redeemed you from there. That is why I command you to do this" (Deut. 24:17-18).

God made it clear to Israel that taking care of the physical needs of widows and orphans, and aliens was not their only responsibility. They were also to make sure that these people were treated fairly and were given the same protection as anyone else. Furthermore, people were not to take away their necessities of life—such as a cloak—in turn for loans to meet other needs.

"When you are harvesting in your field and you overlook a sheaf, do not go back to get it. Leave it for the *alien*, the *fatherless* and the *widow*, so that the Lord your God may bless you in all the work of your hands" (Deut. 24:19).

This was yet another provision for those in need. The Lord gave the same instructions regarding their olive trees and their vineyards. They were not to strip them bare of their produce but were to leave some in order that others' needs might be met.

It is clear from these passages and others in the Old Testament that God was concerned for widows, orphans, and aliens. To violate God's law in this respect would bring judgment upon the children of Israel (Deut. 27:19).

Why these laws? It must be remembered that this was the only means whereby these people could survive. They had no insurance programs, no social security benefits, no old-age pensions, no medicare or unemployment benefits. There were no orphanages or other social institutions to care for the homeless. Israel became a self-contained society, and God's laws for this society outlined the means whereby the widows, orphans, and aliens could be cared for. This then gives us a perspective on the Old Testament culture.

THE NEW TESTAMENT CULTURE

Jesus' Teaching (Mark 12:38-41)

Jesus Christ Himself established continuity between the Old Testament and the New Testament setting. After years of difficulty and dispersion, Israel as a nation still remained intact. Though these people were living under Roman rule, they had freedom to practice their faith. Unfortunately, the religious leaders in Israel in Jesus' day had perverted God's laws. They had developed a legalistic system that benefited themselves and burdened the people. This was particularly true of various groups of religious leaders identified as the Pharisees and the Sadducees.

Jesus minced no words in dealing with their sins. Interestingly, one of their most flagrant sins was to take advantage of the poor—particularly widows. Thus, Jesus said— "Watch out for the teachers of the law . . . . They *devour widows' houses* . . . . Such men will be punished most severely" (Mark 12:38,40).

Here Jesus was chiding the religious leaders for violating a very important aspect of God's Law. They were to see to it that widows were cared for and protected, not abused and used. And what made matters worse, they— the *teachers of the law*—were the ones who were taking advantage of these people with limited means. Jesus let them know that those who perverted the law in this regard would be judged by the law. For this offense they would be "punished most severely."

Ironically, to make His point even more graphic, Jesus at that moment sat down and watched people come into the Temple to put "money into the temple treasury." Mark records that "many rich people threw in large amounts," which, of course, they should have. However, standing in line among the rich folk was "a poor widow." She "put in two very small copper coins," worth very little. However, what she gave was all she had.

Jesus used this live illustration to make a point to His disciples. "I tell you the truth," He said. "This poor widow has put more into the treasury than all the others. They all gave out of their wealth; but she, out of her poverty, put in everything—all she had to live on" (Mark 12:43-44).

Though Jesus was dealing with specific problems at that time, His concern is clear: God's laws have not changed. He had deep concern for those in need—particularly widows, and He had very little patience with those who took advantage of the poor.

These events recorded in the Gospels help us to understand more fully what James had in mind when he wrote—"Religion that God our Father accepts as pure and blameless is this: to look after orphans and widows in their distress." He was writing primarily to Jewish Christians who would understand very well what was happening in the religious community they had been a part of all their lives. This is why he said what he did just a few lines later in his letter: "Listen, my dear brothers: Has not God chosen those who are poor in the eyes of the world to be rich in faith and to inherit the kingdom he promised those who love him? But you have insulted the poor" (Jas. 2:5-6). Some of these people's past behavior toward the poor— the behavior Jesus had condemned—had carried over into their new religious experience as Christians. And this— both Jesus and James said—"ought not to be."

The Church in Jerusalem (Acts 6:1-7)

The next major event recorded in Scripture that deals with the physical needs of widows happened in the church in Jerusalem. Jews had come to Jerusalem from all over the New Testament world for an annual celebration that lasted for fifty days. Among these people were widows who had no doubt used all their savings to make this trip and to spend time in Jerusalem with their friends and relatives, worshiping and thanking God for His goodness to them.

On the final day—the fiftieth day—which was called the day of Pentecost, an unusual event occurred. Unexpectedly, the Holy Spirit came, just as Jesus said He would, and the church was born. With limited knowledge of God's prophetic timetable, it seems that most of the Grecian Jews, rather than returning to their homes in other parts of the world, decided to stay in Jerusalem and to wait for Christ to return and set up His kingdom. In the meantime, the apostles organized a semi-communal society. Those Jews who lived in Jerusalem, identified in Scripture as the "Aramaic-speaking community" (Acts 6:1), voluntarily cared for these people who had come from other parts of the world.

The church grew and expanded rapidly. As we might expect, some people were eventually neglected in the "daily distribution of food"—particularly the widows who had come from other locations. Consequently, a special committee consisting of seven men was appointed to solve this problem. Though the system was temporary, the needs of those neglected were met and God continued to bless the church in Jerusalem. In fact, we read, "So the word of God spread. The number of disciples in Jerusalem increased rapidly, and a large number of priests became obedient to the faith" (Acts 6:7).

The Church in Ephesus

The next major portion of Scripture having to do with widows appears in a letter Paul wrote to Timothy, who had remained in Ephesus to help establish the church. In this passage Paul outlines rather specifically how to deal with the problems they were facing.

First of all, family members were responsible to care for their own. (1 Tim. 5:3-8). This was Paul's first point—and it is clearly stated—"But if a widow has children or grandchildren, these should learn first of all to put their religion into practice by caring for their own family and so repaying their parents and grandparents, for this is pleasing to God" (Eph. 5:4). And then, to underscore the seriousness of violating this biblical guideline, Paul said, "If anyone does not provide for his relatives and especially for his immediate family, he has denied the faith and is worse than an unbeliever" (1 Tim. 5:8).

Only widows who measured up to certain qualifications were to be cared for by the church on a regular basis. (1 Tim. 5:9-10). At this point Paul was even more specific. In addition to having no other source of income, he outlined eight additional criteria.

1. She must be over sixty.
2. She must have been faithful to her husband (morally pure).
3. She must be well known for her good deeds.
4. She should have brought up children.
5. She must be hospitable.
6. She must be willing to wash the feet of saints (a servant at heart).
7. She must be helping those in trouble.
8. She must devote herself to all kinds of good deeds.

It is clear from this list of qualifications that Paul is dealing with cultural needs. But underlying his specific cultural guidelines are supracultural principles. The church is responsible to help care for older people who are indeed living Christlike lives, who have demonstrated their commitment to Christ over a period of time, and who have no other source of income.

Younger widows were encouraged to remarry and to once again establish a home (1 Tim. 5:11-15). Again we see specific cultural needs. Some of what Paul wrote in this paragraph is not easily explained. However, his general points are clear. Widows who were cared for by the church were to devote their time to serving the church. If younger widows were given this privilege, they would be immediately subject to various temptations—sexual desire (1 Tim. 5:11); a tendency to use their time to gossip (1 Tim. 5:13); and a temptation to get into other people's affairs in ways that would create problems (1 Tim. 5:13). Consequently, Paul wrote, "So I counsel younger widows to marry, to have children, to manage their homes and to give the enemy no opportunity for slander" (1 Tim. 5:14).

APPLYING JAMES'S TEACHINGS TODAY

This survey of what the Bible teaches both in the Old and New Testaments yields some clear supracultural principles that can guide the twentieth-century church in helping people who have physical needs. Furthermore, if these principles are supracultural—and I believe they are—they will guide the church no matter where that church is located in the world. Cultural factors may vary, but God's eternal principles help Christians make decisions no matter what the specific cultural setting.

First, God wants His children to care for people who have physical needs that cannot be met in any other way. The overall perspective of Scripture shows that the Lord expressed a specific concern for widows and orphans. However, in the Old Testament He included "aliens." In the New Testament Paul wrote, "Therefore, as we have opportunity, *let us do good to all people, especially to those who belong to the family of believers*" (Gal. 6:10).

Northwest Bible Church in Dallas demonstrated this principle beautifully on one occasion. One missionary couple supported by the church faced a serious crisis overseas when the wife was involved in a serious automobile accident. Facing the effects of a serious head injury, Jill lay unconscious in a hospital in Rome, Italy. The prognosis was that she may not live. The church immediately flew the senior pastor to be with Jill and her husband and family. While there, the pastor was told that her only chance of recovery was to fly her to the United States for more advanced medical care. The pastor returned to the church, reported on the problem and asked the congregation for $15,000—the amount needed to bring Jill home. That week the people gave $30,000—twice the amount asked for.

This was love in action! If James could comment on that event, I'm sure he would say, "That was pure and faultless religion."

The Scriptures then are clear that the church has a *special* responsibility for helping Christians in need, but we should not bypass our opportunity to minister to the physical needs of non-Christians as well.

Second, under ordinary circumstances, family members (fathers, mothers, children and relatives) are, first of all, responsible to care for other family members. This principle is clear from Paul's instructions to Timothy. The church should not be burdened with these needs when it is possible for other family members to care for the physical needs of their blood relatives.

Third, needy people who receive regular financial assistance from the church should be committed Christians, having demonstrated Christlike behavior for a lengthy period of time, and with no other source of income to meet their needs. Again, this principle is clear from Paul's letter to Timothy. The qualifications for widows who were "really in need" were very specific and very high. We can rightly assume this would be true of any Christian who had similar needs.

Fourth, the local church is responsible in any given cul-

ture to develop a suitable and appropriate means whereby those who have real needs are assisted and helped. Furthermore, the dispersion of resources should be carefully supervised and managed in harmony with the foregoing supracultural principles and guidelines.

Why is this important? First, every cultural situation calls for different methods. The Old Testament setting involved tithes of food and grain. It involved leaving food in the fields or on the vines so that the poor could survive. In Jerusalem a special committee supervised the distribution of food; and the church in Ephesus required a more sophisticated system. Thus, every cultural situation and every moment in history dictates a need for a unique form or structure to meet physical needs.

Second, standards must be set up because there is within us all a tendency to take advantage of others. Our sinful nature, even as Christians, rears its ugly head more quickly than at any other time when we have personal, physical needs. Consequently, the leaders of the church have the responsibility to make sure that the principles of Scripture are not violated, particularly when dispersing funds that have been made available for needy people.

A PRACTICAL EXAMPLE

In our own church, where I serve as senior pastor, we have set up what we have called a love fund, designed specifically to meet the needs of those who have physical needs. People are encouraged to designate money to this fund, and when needs arise, certain staff pastors are authorized by the elders to approve the dispensing of these funds in the light of certain biblical guidelines. Obviously, this is a twentieth-century form that is suitable for a typical American church. However, in some cultures—even in some places in America—it would be appropriate to also include gifts of food and clothing as well as money.

Specific Guidelines

1. Every effort is made to operate this fund in harmony with government standards. According to IRS regulations, it is not appropriate to give money to the church and to designate that the gift be used for certain individuals—*if* the donor desires a tax deduction from the government. That kind of designation is considered illegal when tax benefits are involved.

However it is *not* illegal to give money to the church and at the same time to bring to the attention of the leaders of the church that someone has a financial need. A judgment can then be made regarding the amount to be given to the needy individual.

2. The elders have authorized the staff pastors to dispense funds when needed, and gifts distributed are reflected in the regular financial reports at monthly board meetings.

3. Every effort is made to answer the following questions before funds are distributed:

Is this indeed a need?

I have known of Christians who conveyed to the church that they had physical needs. Upon investigation it was discovered that they had savings and investments they didn't want to draw upon to meet their own emergencies. It would certainly be a violation of scriptural guidelines to dispense funds to these people; they would be receiving money for their own use that may have been sacrificially given by people who had no savings or investments at all.

If there is indeed a need, are there family members or relatives who can care for this need?

There are Christians who have serious needs who hesitate to make their needs known to other family members.

Or there are family members who could care for needs but who do not take the responsibility, even when they know there is a need.

Church leaders have the responsibility to communicate to both parties the biblical perspective. It would be unfair to those in need, to those who are responsible to help with the need, and to those who have provided money in the church to meet needs, not to follow biblical guidelines.

Is the one in need qualified spiritually to receive help?

This is a more difficult question to answer because there are levels of need and levels of assistance. For example, dispensing a small amount of money on a one-time basis is far different from giving large amounts or regular amounts on a consistent basis. However, Christian leaders are responsible to be good stewards of God's money even when dispensing one-time gifts.

Let me illustrate. A man and his wife stopped by the church office one day. They introduced themselves as Christians who were having car trouble. They lived in another city and said they did not have enough money to get their car fixed. They told me they had heard from another pastor in Dallas that our church was a loving church and we might be able to help them (my first clue that something might not be quite right).

This kind of encounter always puts a pastor in a difficult position. In moments like that I always think of a Scripture in Hebrews which says, "Do not forget to entertain strangers, for by so doing some people have entertained angels without knowing it" (Heb. 13:2).

In that particular situation I had the authority to request a check from the church love fund. But how was I to know who these people were, whether or not they were telling the truth, whether or not there really was a

need, etc.? After talking for a few minutes I asked the man

where he worked. Part of the story, you see, was that he would be getting his next paycheck when he returned to this city and he would then repay the money. He mentioned the company and his immediate superiors. I then asked for the phone number and offered to let him make a long-distance call on our church phone, at no charge to him, to his boss to see if it would be possible for the company to advance him some money to get out of this jam.

At that moment I struck a nerve. The couple immediately accused me of being non-Christian and unloving. They stomped out of my office in a huff. Though I may be wrong, my conclusion was that they were going from church to church with this story in order to get money. Unfortunately, they probably were doing pretty well.

It must be added at this juncture that over the years I have known very few Christians who have taken advantage of our love fund. In fact, on occasion the opposite is true. We have to actually encourage people in need to receive help.

4. When funds are distributed, those receiving help are encouraged to eventually help someone else—when or if this is ever possible.

On very few occasions do we ever give money with any "strings attached." At times we have made interest-free loans to help people in a crisis with the understanding that we will be paid back. But generally the money is given freely with the suggestion that if they can ever help someone else they should consider replacing the money in our love fund to meet someone else's need. In this way they will experience the blessing of giving as well as receiving.

13

What Kind of Religion Does God Accept?—Part II

Religion that God our Father accepts as pure and faultless is this: to look after orphans and widows in their distress and to keep oneself from being polluted by the world (James 1:27).

A pastor once visited a coal mining district and noticed the town appeared very dingy. The coal dust was everywhere—on buildings, trees, shrubs, everything. But as he was walking with one of the foremen he noticed a beautiful white flower. Its petals were as pure as if it were blooming in a daisy field. "The owner of this plant must take very special care of it," said the pastor, "otherwise, it would not be so free from dust and dirt!"

"No," said the foreman. He then took up a handful of coal dust and threw it over the flower. Dust immediately fell off and left the flower as stainless as before. "This plant has an enamel," the foreman explained, "which prevents any dust from clinging to it. I think it must have been created for such a place as this."

The pastor, of course, had a beautiful illustration. This is the kind of Christian we should be in the midst of a sinful and perverted world in which we live. Dirt can be all around us, but if we keep the right "spiritual enamel" on us, the dirt won't stick.

In many respects this is one of the themes that runs through James's epistle. He was vitally concerned that a Christian live a certain kind of life—a life free from worldly influence and contamination. This we've seen clearly in our study thus far. And all of us know, of course, that living for Christ in this world is in some respects like living in a coal mining town with dust and dirt everywhere. It has been that way ever since Adam and Eve introduced sin into the world. Thus James says, "Religion that God our Father accepts as pure and faultless is this: . . . to keep oneself from being polluted by the world" (Jas. 1:27).

This leads us to a very important question. What does James actually mean by "the world"?

THE WORLD

New Testament Words

There are two Greek words in the New Testament that are frequently translated "world." The first is *aion*. This word is translated "world" thirty-two times in the King James version. In the *New International Version* it is often translated "age," which is a more accurate rendering since this word often refers to a *period* or *age*.

For example, compare Galatians 1:4:

King James	New International Version
"Who gave himself for our sins, that he might deliver us from this present evil world, according to the will of God and our Father."	"Who [Jesus Christ] gave himself for our sins to rescue us from the present evil *age,* according to the will of our God and Father."

The second Greek word, *kosmos,* is translated "world" over 170 times. This word refers to the "ordered world" or the "world system." Though in some instances these two Greek words (*aion* and *kosmos*) seem to be used interchangeably, the word *kosmos* is used more often to refer to that "external framework of material *things* and *influences* which tend to affect man adversely in his endeavors for moral integrity and purity."[1] This is the word James used in chapter 1, verse 27.

John's Definition

The apostle John clarifies what James had in mind more specifically than any other New Testament writer. He used the word *kosmos* six times in three succinct verses, 1 John 2:15-17. In verse 15 he says, "Do not love the *world* or anything in the *world.* If anyone loves the *world,* the love of the Father is not in him."

When John exhorted Christians to *"not* love the world or anything in the world," he was *not* saying we should not enjoy the good things God has made. In fact, James himself stated that "every good and perfect gift is from above, coming down from the Father of the heavenly lights" (Jas. 1:17). And Moses wrote that after God created the earth, the land, and the sea, He "saw that it was *good*" (Gen. 1:9). And with each successive day of creation, "God saw that it was *good*" (Gen. 1:12; 1:18; 1:21; 1:25). And when He had finished *all* of His creation, "God saw *all* that he had made, and it was *very good*" (Gen. 1:31).

Unfortunately, Adam and Eve introduced sin into this good and perfect world God created. Ever since that day the "whole creation has been groaning as in the pains of childbirth" (Rom. 8:22). Sin affected the whole universe. Satan became "the ruler of the kingdom of the air, the spirit who is now at work in those who are disobedient" (Eph. 2:2). All mankind was born with the capacity and tendency to pervert and misuse God's good and perfect gifts.

What then was John referring to when he wrote, "Do not love the *world* or anything in the *world*"? The most basic way in which we misuse God's gifts is to focus our affections on them, making them more important than God, the One who gave them. This is why Jesus said on one occasion, "No one can serve two masters. Either he will hate the one and love the other, or he will be devoted to the one and despise the other." And then Jesus gave a specific illustration. "You cannot serve both God and Money" (Matt. 6:24).

In this instance Jesus was not teaching that money or, more generally, material things per se are evil. Rather He was saying that we should not replace God with material possessions. And though it appears that Jesus was presenting an either-or proposition with this example, in reality all of us fall somewhere on a continuum between putting God first or putting material possessions first. The more we put God first, the more our material possessions are in proper perspective and the less we are in bondage to the world. Material things then for the Christian should become a means for glorifying God. When we use them and enjoy them in that sense, we are not loving them.

"For everything in the *world*—the cravings of sinful man, the lust of his eyes, the boasting of what he has and does—comes not from the Father but from the *world*" (1 John 2:16). Here John becomes more specific. Someone has summarized his references to the world in the following way:

"The cravings of sinful man"—base desires

"The lust of the eyes"—false values

"Boasting of what he has and does"—egoism

The Bible often speaks of "evil desire." As James has reminded us, it is at the root of temptation and sin (Jas. 1:14). Thus John, when he spoke of the world, was also speaking of "evil desire" and "cravings." And notice further that John referred to the "cravings of *sinful* man." All of us have desires and cravings which are not wrong per se. But they become worldly or evil when we allow ourselves to use them in sinful ways.

Furthermore, our "eyes" more than any other organ in our bodies become the windows to our soul. What we see often precipitates evil desire. When Eve "*saw* that the fruit of the tree was good for food and pleasing to the *eye*, . . . she took some and ate it" (Gen. 3:6). Sin, therefore, was introduced into the world not because of *what* she saw but because what she saw caused her to violate God's will.

"Pride," or as the *NIV* translates it, "boasting of what he has and does," is at the root of many sinful actions. Not only did Eve *see* that the fruit "was good for food and pleasing to the eye," but she also saw that it was "desirable for gaining wisdom." In her heart she wanted to be more like God in terms of His authority and power and knowledge. And ever since that day man has been trying to prove how great he really is.

"The *world* and its desires pass away, but the man who does the will of God lives forever" (1 John 2:17). John then gives us a criteria for evaluating "the world" and how to relate to it in proper ways. But he also reminds us that the world—even the good gifts in the world—will pass away. There is no salvation for a man who puts his trust in himself, other people, and material things. But if we follow God's will—putting Him first and putting our faith in His Son for salvation—we will not pass away. We will live forever.

Paul's Statements

The apostle Paul also made a number of statements about the "world" that help us understand what James and John had in mind.

For example, to the Corinthians Paul wrote: "Where is the wise man? Where is the scholar? Where is the philosopher of this age? Has not God made foolish the *wisdom of the world*?" (1 Cor. 1:20).

To the Ephesians Paul said, "In which you used to live when you followed the *ways of this world* and of the ruler of the kingdom of the air, the spirit who is now at work in those who are disobedient" (Eph. 2:2).

And to the Colossians, "See to it that no one takes you captive through hollow and deceptive philosophy, which depends on human tradition and the basic *principles of this world* rather than on Christ" (Col. 2:8).

In these verses, Paul used three phrases that describe the world's system—

• "The *wisdom* of the world"
• "The *ways* of this world"
• "The basic *principles* of this world."

In essence, these are the same statements. Whether we use the words *wisdom, ways* or *principles,* we mean a philosophy of life that is man-centered rather than God-centered; a life-style that is selfish rather than unselfish, and that feeds the flesh rather than the spirit. In short, the world system is controlled by Satan's influence rather than the Lord's.

Over the years man has developed many philosophical systems, both religious and secular. Very few put God in the center. And very few lead men and women towards holiness and godliness and provide ultimate answers to life.

I remember a Bible professor I had while in graduate school at Wheaton College who made a profound impact on my own life. His name is Merrill Tenney and he was teaching a course on the Gospel of John. One day he was sharing about a time in his life when he was searching for truth.

Dr. Tenney has a brilliant mind and he began to use his intellectual capabilities to study the writings of numerous philosophers. But in all of his searching he found no ultimate answers until he came back to one simple, profound statement made by Jesus Christ Himself: "I am the way and the truth and the life" (John 14:6). As he shared this experience with us I was deeply moved, for I too had been searching for meaning in life.

The *"wisdom* of the world" has not provided man with answers. The *"ways* of the world" do not ultimately satisfy man's longings for peace and contentment. And the "basic *principles* of this world" lead man not to peace and security but to ultimate chaos and destruction. All history points to these facts.

THE EFFECTS OF THE WORLD

James warns that a Christian should keep himself from "being *polluted* by the world." How can a Christian keep this from happening?

Paul helps us with the answer to this question in his letter to the Romans. "Do not *conform* any longer to the *pattern of this world,"* he wrote, "but be *transformed* by the renewing of your mind" (Rom. 12:2).

We all live in this world. It surrounds us and touches our lives every day. There is no escaping its reality. Furthermore, God does not want us to leave the world until He removes us (1 Cor. 5:10). Jesus said, "You are the *salt* of the earth . . . . You are the *light of the world*" (Matt. 5:13-14). We are to change the world—not to allow the world to change us.

Unfortunately, the opposite is often true. We let the world's system press us into its mold. I remember on one occasion visiting a large automobile manufacturing plant where they used large presses to make certain parts of cars. Large sheets of metal were heated until they were soft and pliable and then inserted into these large presses. As each press was lowered onto the molten metal, it literally conformed each piece into its mold. As the metal cooled, it once again hardened. However, it was no longer a simple piece of metal. It was a unique part of an automobile.

Just so, Paul implies that the world system is like a large press. As Christians, however, we must not allow the world to press us into its mold. This is the thrust of Paul's statement in Romans 12:2, "Do not conform any longer to the pattern of this world."

And it need not happen. It is the will of God that we "become blameless and pure, children of God without fault in a crooked and depraved . . . universe" (Phil. 2:15).

If this *is* God's will—and it is—how then can we practice this kind of religion?

LIVING FOR CHRIST IN A SINFUL WORLD?

James lays before us a foundational key in practicing this kind of religion. Every Christian is *"to keep oneself from being polluted by the world."*

God does not take a Christian by the scruff of the neck and rescue him from worldly temptation and sin. We are responsible for ourselves! To practice holiness we must obey Christ. We must avoid situations that drag us down and taint our lives.

Some Exhortations

Note how our responsibility is focused in the following injunctions:

• *"Do not conform any longer to the pattern of this world,* but be transformed by the renewing of your mind"* (Rom. 12:2).

• *"See to it that no one takes you captive through hollow, deceptive philosophy,* which depends on human tradition and the basic principles of this world rather than on Christ" (Col. 2:8).

• "You adulterous people, don't you know that friendship with the world is hatred toward God? *Anyone who chooses to be a friend of the world becomes an enemy of God"* (Jas. 4:4).

• *"Do not love the world or anything in the world"* (1 John 2:15).

• *"Keep yourself pure"* (1 Tim. 5:22).

• *"It [God's grace] teaches us to say 'No' to ungodliness and worldly passions,* and to live self-controlled, upright and godly lives in this present age" (Tit. 2:12).

These are just a few specific exhortations that make it clear that every Christian is responsible to keep himself from "being polluted by the world."

The other dimension to this, however, is that God does not expect us to do it on our own strength. He has given us divine resources to enable us to carry out His commandments.

Listen to the apostle Peter: "His divine power has given us everything we need for life and godliness through our knowledge of him who called us by his own glory and goodness. Through these he has given us his very great and precious promises, so that through them you may participate in the divine nature and *escape the corruption in the world* caused by evil desires" (2 Pet. 1:3-4).

A Process

Conforming to Christ's life is a process. That is why Paul stated, "Be transformed by the renewing of your mind." This process varies with different people. Some individuals have conformed their lives to the world's pattern for years. And for some it *takes years,* even after conversion to Christ, to conform their lives to the Lord. Old habits do not disappear overnight. But they can and must disappear. We *can* change! We *must* change if we are to be obedient to Christ and to love Him as He has loved us.

The key is our "mind" and "inner being." Paul states that transformation takes place "by the renewing" of the "mind." And that renewal comes primarily through reprogramming our minds and hearts with God's truth.

Paul wrote to the Philippians, "Finally, brothers, whatever is true, whatever is noble, whatever is right, whatever is pure, whatever is lovely, whatever is admirable—if anything is excellent or praiseworthy—*think about such things*" (Phil. 4:8).

TWENTIETH-CENTURY CHRISTIAN LIFE-STYLE

Ever since the time of Christ His followers have struggled against the influence of the world. The New Testament letters particularly are a graphic portrayal of this struggle. Being conformed to Christ's image in all aspects of life has never been automatic or instantaneous.

Twentieth-century Christians struggle too. We're *all* in process. And many of our problems are identical to first-century Christians. This should not surprise us, because people are people no matter where they live on this earth and no matter in what period of history. There has been one constant in history—the "old nature" in us all.

There are unique differences, however, in the world environment. For instance, take the American culture versus the New Testament culture. When Jesus appeared on earth the world system was very degenerate. People worshiped false gods, and immorality and every other kind of sin was rampant. Even Judaism had deteriorated rapidly under the influence of the Greek and Roman life-style. The message of Christianity began to penetrate this system, introducing a new life-style patterned after God's laws of holiness and righteousness.

On the other hand, when America was founded it was built upon the Hebrew-Christian ethic. Though we were never a Christian nation in the true sense of that word, we were a nation built upon biblical values which influenced our relationship with one another in business, in social relationships, and in the world of recreation and entertainment. In many respects, biblical values and our cultural values overlapped. For example, the way a Christian did business was very little different from how a non-Christian did business. Basically, both were committed to honesty and integrity (see fig. 1).

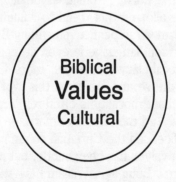

And then something happened. In the twentieth century a dramatic shift took place (see fig. 2). Our cultural values began to change. In some respects there is very little overlap between biblical values and our cultural values. In fact, many Americans no longer believe in absolutes of any kind.

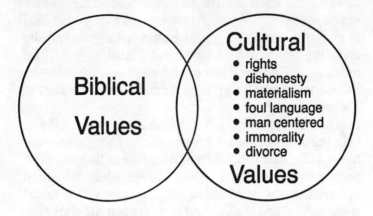

Today there are many reflections of the world, even in the life-style of many Christians. The strong emphasis on personal rights has introduced an egocentric approach to living—a me-ism that is self-centered. Lying and cheating have become the norm in business dealings, and some Christians have allowed this trend to influence their own lives. Materialism is rampant, even among Bible-believing Christians. And foul language is even creeping into some evangelicals' vocabulary. More and more Christians are also following the sexual ethics of this world. What the Bible teaches about morality is often reinterpreted or not taken seriously. And the impact of marriage breakups has dramatically influenced the Christian community.

This shift in values has been subtle, but it is very real. We are all victims. Long ago, William Law warned that the world is now a greater enemy to the Christian than it was in apostolic times. He believes it is a greater enemy because it has greater power over Christians through favors, riches, honors, rewards, and protection than it had by the fire and fury of the Christians' persecutors. Furthermore, the world is a more dangerous enemy by having lost its appearance of enmity. Its outward profession of Christianity makes it no longer appear as an enemy, and therefore the people are easily persuaded to resign themselves to be governed and directed by it.

In view of the trends in our culture, it is time that all Christians take seriously James's statement, "Religion that God our Father accepts as pure and faultless is this: . . . to keep oneself from being polluted by the world" (Jas. 1:27).

LIFE RESPONSE

Evaluate your life in the light of God's standard of righteousness. Are there any areas in your life where you are allowing yourself to "be conformed to the pattern of this world," or are you "being transformed by the renewing of your mind"? What specific areas of your life need particular attention?

John Wesley once said, "Anything that cools my love for Christ is the world."

John Newton had a life rule: "I make a rule of Christian duty never to go to a place where there is not room for my Master as well as myself."

Sign in a church vestibule: "If you were on trial for being a Christian, would there be enough evidence to convict you?"

Note

1. Spiros Zodhiates, *The Behavior of Belief* (Grand Rapids: Wm. B. Eerdmans Publishing Co., 1959), p. 144.

Center for Church Renewal

The local church is God's primary social unit in the world ... however, the church includes smaller interrelated units: the family, the marriage and the individual.

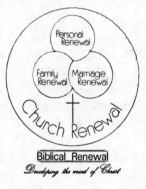

Can you identify where the greatest need is in the Christian community today:

> in the church?
> in the family?
> in marriage?
> in personal Christian living?

The Center for Church Renewal exists to help bring biblical renewal to every segment of the Christian community.

For more information, write:
Center for Church Renewal
Box 863173
Plano, TX 75086